moda BLOCK HEADS

48 Quilt-Along Blocks Plus Settings for Finished Quilts

LISA BONGEAN ◆ BETSY CHUTCHIAN
LYNNE HAGMEIER ◆ JO MORTON
JAN PATEK ◆ CARRIE NELSON

Martingale®
Create with Confidence

Moda Blockheads:
48 Quilt-Along Blocks Plus Settings for Finished Quilts
© 2018 by Martingale & Company®

Martingale®
19021 120th Ave. NE, Ste. 102
Bothell, WA 98011-9511 USA
ShopMartingale.com

Printed in China
23 22 21 20 19 18   8 7 6 5 4 3 2 1

Library of Congress Cataloging-in-Publication Data

Title: Moda blockheads : 48 quilt-along blocks plus settings for finished quilts.
Description: Bothell, WA : Martingale & Company, 2018.
Identifiers: LCCN 2018031423 | ISBN 9781604689778
Subjects: LCSH: Patchwork--Patterns. | Quilting--Patterns. | Patchwork quilts.
Classification: LCC TT835 .M5925 2018 | DDC 746.46/041--dc23
LC record available at https://lccn.loc.gov/2018031423

MISSION STATEMENT

We empower makers who use fabric and yarn to make life more enjoyable.

CREDITS

**PUBLISHER AND
CHIEF VISIONARY OFFICER**
Jennifer Erbe Keltner

CONTENT DIRECTOR
Karen Costello Soltys

DESIGN MANAGER
Adrienne Smitke

MANAGING EDITOR
Tina Cook

PRODUCTION MANAGER
Regina Girard

ACQUISITIONS EDITOR
Amelia Johanson

PHOTOGRAPHER
Brent Kane

TECHNICAL EDITOR
Nancy Mahoney

ILLUSTRATOR
Sandy Loi

COPY EDITOR
Durby Peterson

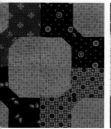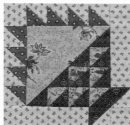

CONTENTS

INTRODUCTION 5

QUILT GALLERY 7

QUILT BLOCKS 15

Block 1: Aunt Dinah 16

Block 2: Four X 17

Block 3: Whirligig 18

Block 4: Bee Skep 20

Block 5: Coronation 22

Block 6: Turnstile 24

Block 7: Penny Basket 26

Block 8: Square in a Square 29

Block 9: Basket and Flower 30

Block 10: Lisa's Star 32

Block 11: Puzzled 34

Block 12: Ohio Star Variation 36

Block 13: Bow Tie Quartet 37

Block 14: Lawyer's Puzzle 38

Block 15: Flags 40

Block 16: T Block 42

Block 17: Trail of Tears 44

Block 18: Corn No Beans 45

Block 19: Devil's Claw 46

Block 20: Night Flight 47

Block 21: Flying Geese Variation 48

Block 22: Rocky Mountain Puzzle 50

Block 23: Birdhouse 52

Block 24: Winneconne Star 54

Block 25: Twice the Friendship 56

Block 26: Union Variation 58

Block 27: Pumpkin 60

Block 28: Juneau 62

Block 29: Cat's Cradle 64

Block 30: Four Patch Dash 65

Block 31: Dot Dash 66

Block 32: Dutchman's Puzzle 67

Block 33: Starz 68

Block 34: House 70

Block 35: Northridge 72

Block 36: Shoo Dat 74

Block 37: Double Delight Star 76

Block 38: Framed Star 78

Block 39: Cat and Dog 80

Block 40: Basket of Triangles 82

Block 41: Pinwheel Star 84

Block 42: Sunflower 86

Block 43: Any Direction 88

Block 44: Double Dutch 90

Block 45: Cardinal 92

Block 46: Starry Nine Patch 94

Block 47: Honeymoon 96

Block 48: Peace and Plenty 97

QUILT PLANS 99

MEET THE CONTRIBUTORS 112

Introduction

It started as a very simple idea. Let's celebrate traditional quilts and quilters by having five of Moda's fabric designers host a yearlong block-of-the-week program. Every Wednesday one designer would publish a block pattern, and all the other lovely ladies would make that block using reproduction and primitive-style fabrics they loved. Those blocks would eventually become part of the kind of quilt for which each designer was known. It would be fun too!

Sounds easy so far, right? Coming up with a name for this group took a little longer because these are hip, cool, feisty women! *Blockheads.* It's different. So who are they? Lynne Hagmeier of Kansas Troubles Quilters was instrumental in getting this party started. Jan Patek. Lisa Bongean. Jo Morton. Betsy Chutchian. You'll get to know more about each of them through their blocks and tips in the coming pages.

A plan? We didn't have one. The only thing we knew for sure was that we were each making 48 blocks, 6" finished. We'd blog about our blocks each week, sharing ideas or tips. And we'd sew a few variations. A setting? Whatever . . . we'll figure that out later. It was a given that the finished quilts would each be quite different.

That's when the fun started. So many quilters wanted to join in. A Facebook group? Sure! We calculated approximate yardages, shared blocks, and explored alternate piecing methods. Quilters in the group shared tips and offered support and advice. They helped each other solve problems, both the sewing kind and the technical computer kind. And they cheered each other on as blocks were posted to Instagram and Facebook within an hour of each new pattern being published.

It quickly became clear that—regardless of age, experience, or background—it isn't the style of quilt or fabric that brings this community of quilters together, it's the joy of making something. Big or small, simple or complicated, we get to take a little bit of time and stitch a little bit of ourselves into something we create.

It may not be Wednesday when you're reading this, but within the pages of this book, it's always Blockheads Wednesday, and you've got a new block to make!

Happy Wednesday!
Carrie Nelson

Quilt Gallery

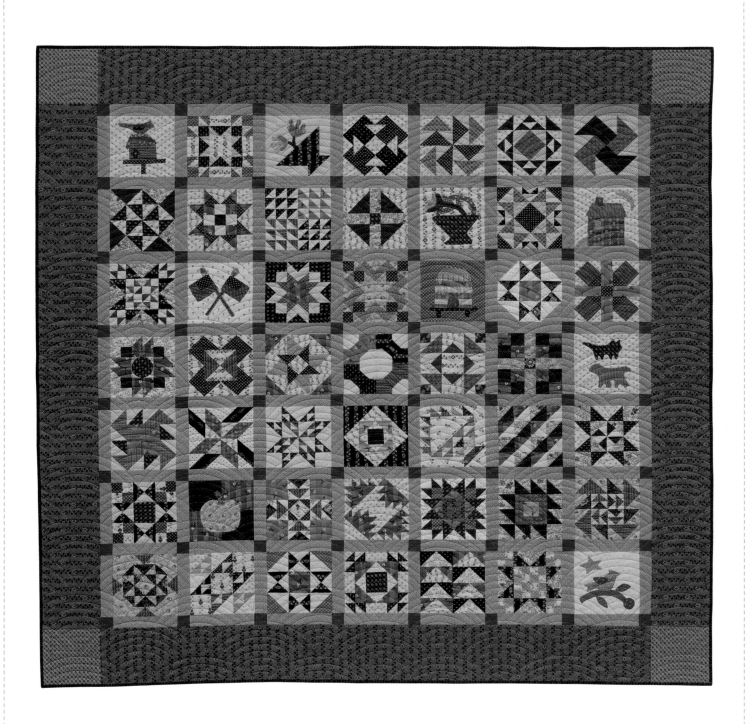

Pieced by Jo Morton; machine quilted by Maggi Honeyman
Finished blocks: 6" × 6"   ◆   Finished quilt: 63½" × 63½"

Pattern instructions can be found on page 102.

Moda Blockheads

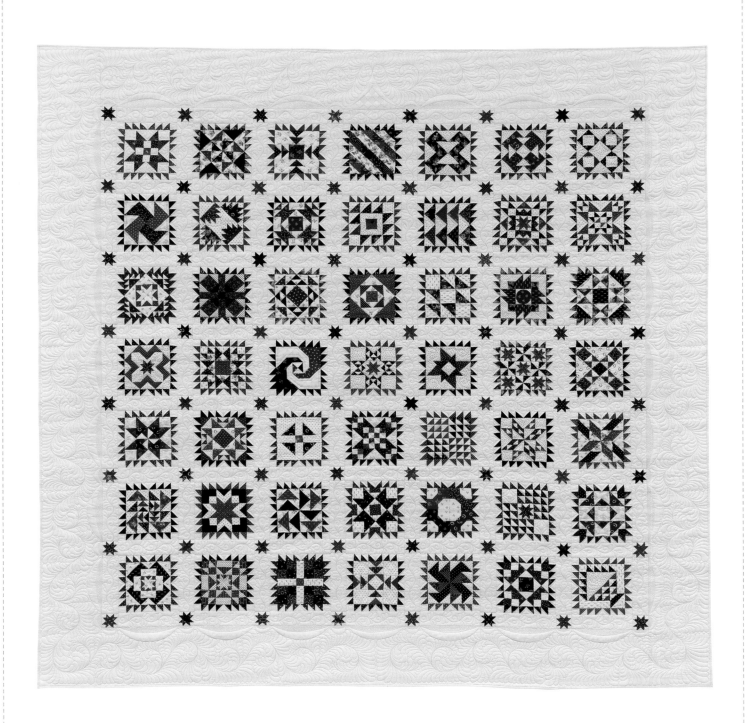

Pieced by Lisa Bongean; machine quilted by Linda Hrcka

Finished blocks: 6" × 6" ◆ Finished quilt: 88½" × 88½"

Pattern instructions can be found on page 108.

Pieced by Betsy Chutchian; machine quilted by Maggi Honeyman
Finished blocks: 6" × 6" ◆ Finished quilt: 63½" × 81½"

Pattern instructions can be found on page 100.

Pieced and appliquéd by Jan Patek; machine quilted by Lori Kukuk

Finished blocks: 6" × 6" ◆ Center appliqué block: 18" × 18" ◆ Finished quilt: 54½" × 60½"

Pattern instructions can be found on page 106.

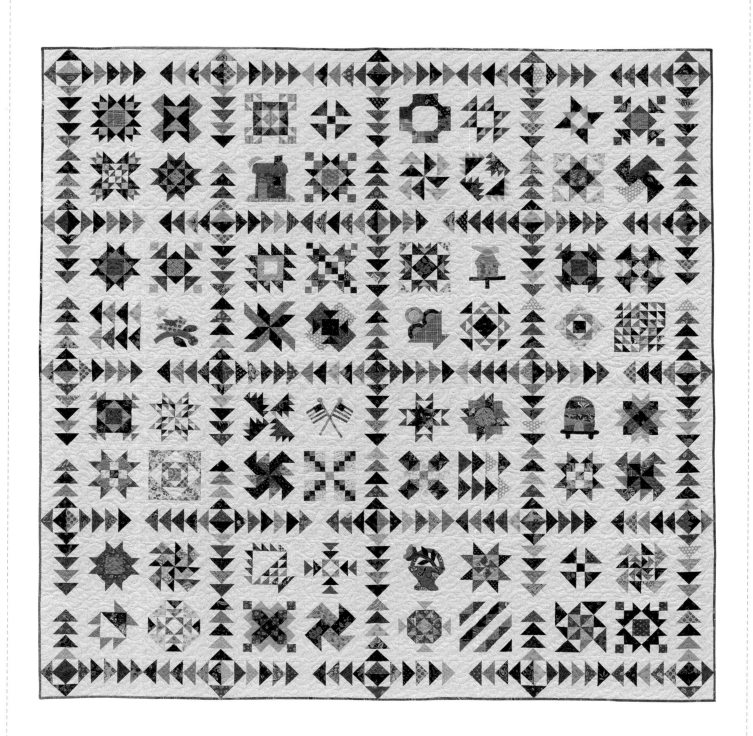

Pieced by Carrie Nelson; machine quilted by Carrie Straka of Red Velvet Quilts

Finished blocks: 6" × 6" ◆ Finished quilt: 77½" × 77½"

Pattern instructions can be found on page 103.

Pieced by Lynne Hagmeier; machine quilted by Joy Johnson of Joyful Quilting
Finished blocks: 6" × 6" ◆ Finished quilt: 102½" × 108½"

Pattern instructions can be found on page 110.

Quilt Blocks

01 AUNT DINAH

by Betsy Chutchian

MATERIALS

The featured block uses 2 light and 3 dark prints.

A: 4 squares, 1⅞" × 1⅞", of light print #1; cut in half diagonally to yield 8 triangles

B: 4 squares, 1½" × 1½", of dark print #1

C: 2 squares, 2⅞" × 2⅞", of dark print #2; cut in half diagonally to yield 4 triangles

D: 1 square, 3¼" × 3¼", of light print #2; cut into quarters diagonally to yield 4 triangles

E: 1 square, 3¼" × 3¼", of dark print #3; cut into quarters diagonally to yield 4 triangles

F: 2 squares, 2⅞" × 2⅞", of light print #1; cut in half diagonally to yield 4 triangles

G: 1 square, 2½" × 2½", of light print #2

BLOCK ASSEMBLY

Press all seam allowances in the directions indicated by the arrows.

1. Sew two A triangles to adjacent sides of a B square. Make four units.

Make 4 units.

2. Sew a C triangle to an A/B unit to make a corner unit. Make four units that measure 2½" square, including seam allowances.

Make 4 units, 2½" × 2½".

3. Sew a D triangle to an E triangle. Make four units.

Make 4 units.

4. Sew an F triangle to each D/E unit to make a side unit. Make four units that measure 2½" square, including seam allowances.

Make 4 units, 2½" × 2½".

5. Lay out the corner units, side units, and G square in three rows, rotating the units as shown. Sew the units and square together into rows. Join the rows to make a block that measures 6½" square, including seam allowances.

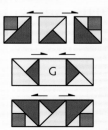 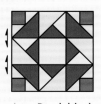

Aunt Dinah block

02 FOUR X

by Jo Morton

MATERIALS

The featured block uses 1 light, 1 dark, and 2 medium prints.

A: 2 squares, 2⅞" × 2⅞", of light print
B: 2 squares, 2⅞" × 2⅞", of medium print #1
C: 2 squares, 3¼" × 3¼", of light print
D: 2 squares, 3¼" × 3¼", of dark print
E: 1 square, 2½" × 2½", of medium print #2

BLOCK ASSEMBLY

Press all seam allowances in the directions indicated by the arrows.

1. Draw a diagonal line from corner to corner on the wrong side of each A square. Place a marked square right sides together with a B square. Sew ¼" from both sides of the drawn line. Cut the unit apart on the marked line to make two half-square-triangle units. Make four units that measure 2½" square, including seam allowances.

Make 4 units,
2½" × 2½".

2. Repeat step 1 using the C and D squares to make four units that measure 2⅞" square, including seam allowances.

Make 4 units,
2⅞" × 2⅞".

3. On the wrong side of two C/D units, draw a diagonal line from corner to corner, perpendicular to the seamline. Layer a marked unit on an unmarked C/D unit, right sides together with the dark triangles on top of the light triangles. Sew ¼" from both sides of the drawn line. Cut on the line to yield two hourglass units. Make four units that measure 2½" square, including seam allowances.

Make 4 units,
2½" × 2½".

4. Lay out the A/B units, hourglass units, and E square in three rows, rotating the units as shown. Sew the units and square together into rows. Join the rows to make a block that measures 6½" square, including seam allowances.

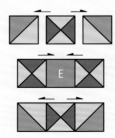 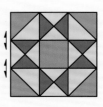

Four X block

03 WHIRLIGIG

by Lynne Hagmeier

MATERIALS

The featured block uses 1 dark, 1 medium, and 2 light prints.

A: 12 squares, 2" × 2", of light print #1
B: 4 rectangles, 2" × 3½", of dark print
C: 4 rectangles, 2" × 3½", of medium print
D: 4 squares, 2" × 2", of light print #2

BLOCK ASSEMBLY

Press all seam allowances in the directions indicated by the arrows.

1. Layer an A square on one end of a B rectangle, right sides together and raw edges aligned. Stitch diagonally across the A square. (You can draw a line diagonally from corner to corner or just eyeball it.) Trim the seam allowances to ¼"; press. Layer a second A square on the opposite end of the B rectangle. Sew, trim, and press. Make four units that measure 2" × 3½".

Make 4 units,
2" × 3½".

2. In the same way, sew an A and a D square on a C rectangle as shown. Trim the seam allowances to ¼". Make four units that measure 2" × 3½".

Make 4 units,
2" × 3½".

3. Sew a unit from step 1 to each unit from step 2 to make four quarter-block units. The units should measure 3½" square, including seam allowances.

Make 4 units,
3½" × 3½".

4. Lay out the units in two rows, rotating them as shown. Sew the units together into rows. Join the rows to make a block that measures 6½" square, including seam allowances.

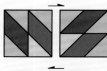 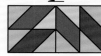 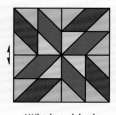

Whirligig block

Layered Patchwork Whirligig Block

LAYERED PATCHWORK

Layered Patchwork, Lynne's unique method of layering and topstitching cut pieces, simplifies traditional quilt blocks. A dotted line on the diagram indicates topstitching on the layered piece. There's no flipping or pressing toward the corners with this technique. The raw edges are left exposed for a cozy, primitive look.

MATERIALS

The featured block uses 1 dark, 1 medium, and 2 light prints.

A: 6 squares, 2" × 2", of light print #1; cut in half diagonally to yield 12 triangles
B: 4 rectangles, 2" × 3½", of dark print
C: 4 rectangles, 2" × 3½", of medium print
D: 2 squares, 2" × 2", of light print #2; cut in half diagonally to yield 4 triangles
Water-soluble glue stick

BLOCK ASSEMBLY

1. Glue baste two A triangles on one B rectangle, right sides facing up and 90° corners aligned. Using coordinating thread, topstitch ⅛" from the bias edges of each triangle. Make four units that measure 2" × 3½", including seam allowances.

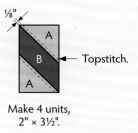

Make 4 units, 2" × 3½".

2. Glue baste an A and a D triangle on a C rectangle, right sides facing up and 90° corners aligned. Using coordinating thread, topstitch ⅛" from the bias edges of each triangle. Make four units that measure 2" × 3½", including seam allowances.

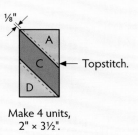

Make 4 units, 2" × 3½".

3. Refer to steps 3 and 4 of "Block Assembly" on page 18 to construct the block.

04 BEE SKEP

by Jan Patek

MATERIALS

The featured block uses 1 light and 3 medium prints.

1 rectangle, 4½" × 5", of light print for bee skep
1 rectangle, 2" × 5", of medium print #1 for
  bee skep base
1 rectangle, 1½" × 2", of medium print #2 for
  bee skep door
1 square, 7" × 7", of medium print #3 for
  background
Embroidery floss
Freezer paper
Appliqué glue (optional)

BLOCK ASSEMBLY

The instructions are written for needle-turn appliqué, which Jan used, but use your favorite method if you prefer. All the appliqué patterns are on page 21. Reverse the patterns for fusible appliqué.

1. Trace the bee skep, base, and door onto the dull side of the freezer paper. Cut out the templates directly on the line.

2. Place each freezer-paper template on the right side of the appropriate fabric, shiny side down. Press in place.

3. Trace around the templates. Cut out the fabric shapes, adding ¼" seam allowance all around. Remove the freezer-paper template.

4. Fold the background square in half in both directions and finger-press to crease.

5. Using the creases as placement guidelines, pin, baste, or glue the pieces to the background, starting with the bee skep base. Appliqué in place. Add the bee skep and then the door.

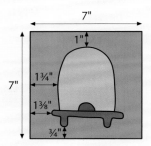

Appliqué placement guide

6. Embroider the lines on the bee skep using two strands of embroidery floss and a stem stitch.

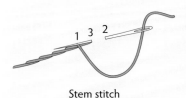

Stem stitch

7. Press the block on the wrong side and trim it to 6½" square, keeping the design centered.

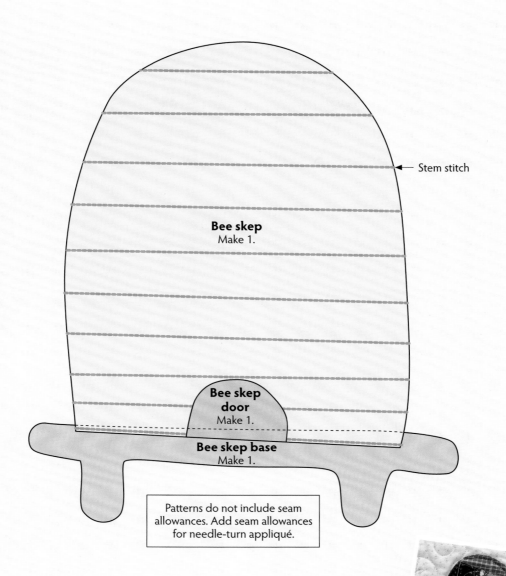

Stem stitch

Bee skep
Make 1.

Bee skep door
Make 1.

Bee skep base
Make 1.

Patterns do not include seam allowances. Add seam allowances for needle-turn appliqué.

" Around the Block

"Rather than embroider lines across one piece of fabric to represent a bee skep, I was inspired (by Jan's work over the years) to do a quasi-improv-pieced skep. I hand-appliquéd this block because I desperately need the practice!"

~ CARRIE NELSON

05 CORONATION

by Lisa Bongean

MATERIALS

The featured block uses 2 light, 2 medium, and 2 dark prints.

A: 5 squares, 1½" × 1½", of light print #1
B: 4 squares, 1½" × 1½", of dark print #1
C: 1 square, 1½" × 1½", of medium print #1
D: 14 squares, 1⅛" × 1½", of light print #1
E: 8 squares, 1⅛" × 1⅛", of dark print #2
F: 4 rectangles, 1⅛" × 1⅝", of light print #1
G: 8 squares, 1⅝" × 1⅝", of medium print #2
H: 4 rectangles, 1⅝" × 2¾", of light print #1
I: 12 squares, 1⅝" × 1⅝", of light print #2
J: 12 squares, 1⅝" × 1⅝", of dark print #1
K: 4 squares, 1¼" × 1¼", of light print #2

BLOCK ASSEMBLY

Press all seam allowances in the directions indicated by the arrows.

1. Draw a diagonal line from corner to corner on the wrong side of each A square. Place a marked square right sides together with a B square. Sew ¼" from both sides of the drawn line. Cut the unit apart on the marked line to make two half-square-triangle units. Make eight units that measure 1⅛" square, including seam allowances.

2. Repeat step 1 using the remaining marked A square and the C square to make two half-square-triangle units that measure 1⅛" square, including seam allowances.

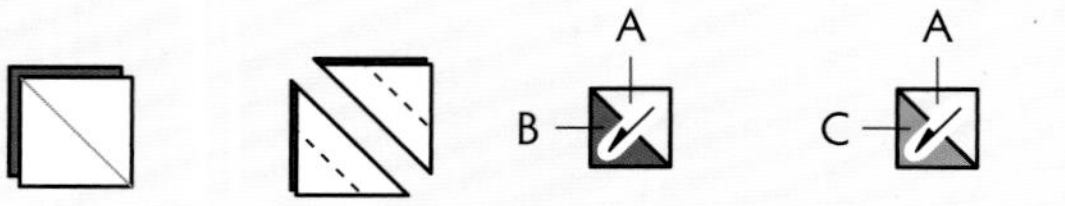

Make 8 units, 1⅛" × 1⅛".   Make 2 units, 1⅛" × 1⅛".

3. Join two A/B half-square-triangle units and two D squares as shown. Make four units. Join the A/C units and two D squares to make one unit. The units should measure 1⅝" square, including seam allowances.

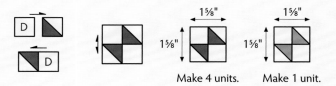

Make 4 units.   Make 1 unit.

4. Layer an E square on one end of an F rectangle, right sides together and raw edges aligned. Stitch diagonally across the E square. (You can draw a line diagonally from corner to corner or just eyeball it.) Trim the seam allowances to ¼"; press. Layer a second marked E square on the opposite end of the rectangle. Sew, trim, and press to make a flying-geese unit. Make four units that measure 1⅛" × 1⅝", including seam allowances.

Make 4 units, 1⅛" × 1⅝".

5. Lay out the A/C/D unit from step 3, the four flying-geese units, and the four remaining D squares in three rows. Sew the units and squares together into rows and press. Join the rows to make the center unit, which should measure 2¾" square, including seam allowances.

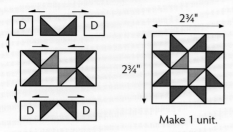

Make 1 unit.

6. Repeat step 4 to sew two G squares on each H rectangle. Make four units that measure 1⅝" × 2¾".

Make 4 units,
1⅝" × 2¾".

7. Lay out the A/B/D units from step 3, the G/H flying-geese units, and the center unit in three rows, rotating them as shown. Sew the units into rows. Join the rows to make a star unit that measures 5" square, including seam allowances.

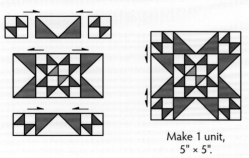

Make 1 unit,
5" × 5".

FITTING FINESSE

The math isn't exact for the center unit, as the units are a little oversized. To avoid cutting off the points, take a slightly wider seam allowance, and it should work out fine. ◆

8. Draw a diagonal line from corner to corner on the wrong side of each I square. Place a marked square right sides together with a J square. Sew ¼" from both sides of the drawn line. Cut the unit apart on the marked line to make two half-square-triangle units. Make 24 units that measure 1¼" square, including seam allowances.

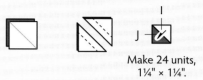

Make 24 units,
1¼" × 1¼".

9. Join six I/J half-square-triangle units to make a side unit, making sure to orient them as shown. Make two units that measure 1¼" × 5", including seam allowances. Join six I/J half-square-triangle units and two K squares to make a top unit that measures 1¼" × 6½", including seam allowances. Repeat to make a bottom unit.

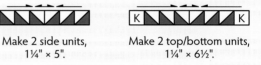

Make 2 side units,
1¼" × 5".

Make 2 top/bottom units,
1¼" × 6½".

10. Sew the side units to opposite sides of the star unit. Sew the top and bottom units to the star unit to make a block that measures 6½" square, including seam allowances.

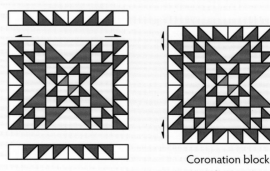

Coronation block

06 TURNSTILE

by Carrie Nelson

MATERIALS

The featured block uses 1 light, 1 medium, and 1 dark print.

A: 1 square, 3¼" × 3¼", of dark print; cut into quarters diagonally to yield 4 triangles (2 will be extra)

B: 1 square, 3¼" × 3¼", of medium print; cut into quarters diagonally to yield 4 triangles (2 will be extra)

C: 8 squares, 2½" × 2½", of light print

D: 2 rectangles, 2½" × 4½", of medium print

E: 2 rectangles, 2½" × 4½", of dark print

BLOCK ASSEMBLY

Press all seam allowances in the directions indicated by the arrows.

1. Join two A and two B triangles as shown to make an hourglass unit. Make one unit that measures 2½" square, including seam allowances.

Make 1 unit,
2½" × 2½".

2. Mark a diagonal line from corner to corner on the wrong side of the C squares. Place a marked square on one end of a D rectangle, right sides together, and stitch on the drawn line. Trim the seam allowances to ¼"; press. Place a second marked square on the opposite end of the rectangle, right sides together; stitch, trim, and press to make a flying-geese unit. Make two units that measure 2½" × 4½", including seam allowances.

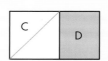 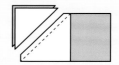

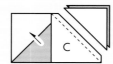 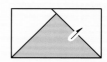

Make 2 units,
2½" × 4½".

3. Repeat step 2 using the remaining marked C squares and the E rectangles to make two units that measure 2½" × 4½", including seam allowances.

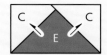

Make 2 units,
2½" × 4½".

4. With a C/D flying-geese unit positioned vertically, place the hourglass unit on the upper-right corner, right sides together. Start stitching at the top edge and stop about 1" from the bottom of the hourglass unit.

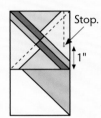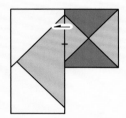

5. Sew a C/E flying-geese unit to the top of the unit from step 4, sewing all the way across the units. Then sew a C/D flying-geese unit to the right side, sewing all the way across.

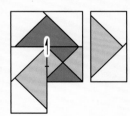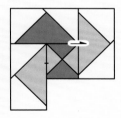

6. Sew a C/E flying-geese unit to the bottom of the unit from step 5. Then finish sewing the open section of the hourglass-unit seam closed to make the block. The block should measure 6½" square, including seam allowances.

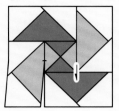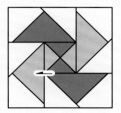

Turnstile block

"

Around the Block

"For a scrappier look, substitute two half-square-triangle units that finish at 2½" square for each flying-geese unit. The result may not look like a turnstile, but it will be fun!"

~ Carrie Nelson

07 PENNY BASKET

by Lynne Hagmeier

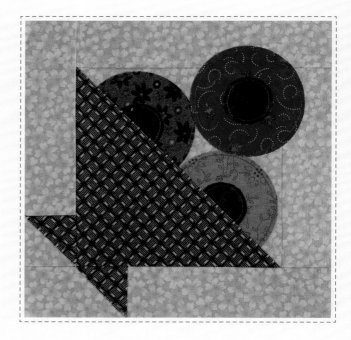

MATERIALS

The featured block uses 1 light, 2 dark, and 3 assorted medium prints.

A: 3 squares, 1¼" × 1¼", of dark print #1
B: 3 squares, 2½" × 2½", of assorted medium prints
C: 1 square, 4⅞" × 4⅞", of light print; cut in half diagonally to yield 2 triangles (1 will be extra)
D: 1 square, 4⅞" × 4⅞", of dark print #2; cut in half diagonally to yield 2 triangles (1 will be extra)
E: 3 rectangles, 1½" × 4½", of light print
F: 1 rectangle, 1½" × 5½", of light print
G: 1 square, 1½" × 1½", of light print
H: 2 squares, 1½" × 1½", of dark print #2
I: 1 rectangle, 1½" × 2½", of light print
5" × 6" rectangle of paper-backed fusible web
Template plastic

BLOCK ASSEMBLY

The appliqué patterns are on page 28; instructions are for fusible appliqué. Press all seam allowances in the directions indicated by the arrows.

1. Trace the flower center pattern three times onto the fusible web, leaving ½" between the shapes. Cut out ¼" outside the drawn lines.

2. Fuse the shapes to the wrong side of the A squares, following the manufacturer's instructions. Cut out the circles on the drawn lines and peel away the paper backing.

3. Trace the penny flower pattern onto template plastic; cut out directly on the line. Use the template to trace a penny flower on the *right side* of each B square. Fuse a flower center in the center of each penny flower.

4. Apply a 2½" square of fusible web on the wrong side of each B square. Cut out the penny flowers on the traced line. Make three penny flowers.

Make 3 units.

5. Fold two penny flowers in half and finger-press to crease the centerline. Measure ¼" below the center crease and trim. Make two half flowers.

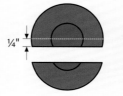

¼"

Make 2 units.

6. Peel away the paper backing from the half flowers and place them on a C triangle, with the raw edges aligned and 1⅛" in from each end as shown. Fuse along the seam allowance only.

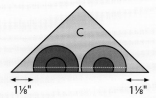

7. Sew the C triangle from step 6 to a D triangle as shown. Press, being careful to *not* touch the iron to the half flowers. The basket unit should measure 4½" square, including seam allowances.

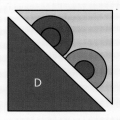 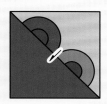

Make 1 unit,
4½" × 4½".

8. Pin the half flowers out of the way. Sew an E rectangle to the right side of the basket unit. Sew the F rectangle to the top of the unit. The basket unit should now measure 5½" square, including seam allowances.

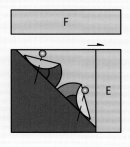 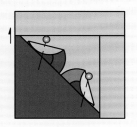

Make 1 unit,
5½" × 5½".

9. Unpin the half flowers and fuse them in place. Using coordinating thread, topstitch ⅛" from the edges of the half flowers and flower centers. Peel away the paper backing from the remaining penny flower and fuse it in place. Topstitch ⅛" from the edge of the flower and flower center.

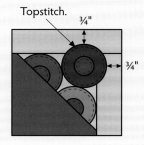

10. Draw a diagonal line from corner to corner on the wrong side of the G square. Place the square right sides together with an H square. Stitch on the drawn line. Trim the seam allowances to ¼"; press. Make one half-square-triangle unit that measures 1½" square, including seam allowances.

Make 1 unit,
1½" × 1½".

11. Sew the half-square-triangle unit to one end of an E rectangle to make a unit that measures 1½" × 5½", including seam allowances.

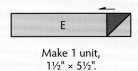

Make 1 unit,
1½" × 5½".

12. Draw a diagonal line from corner to corner on the wrong side of the remaining H square. Place the marked square on one end of the I rectangle, right sides together. Stitch on the drawn line. Trim the seam allowances to ¼"; press. Make one unit that measures 1½" × 2½", including seam allowances.

Make 1 unit,
1½" × 2½".

13. Sew the H/I unit to one end of the remaining E rectangle to make a unit that measures 1½" × 6½", including seam allowances.

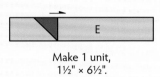

Make 1 unit,
1½" × 6½".

14. Sew the unit from step 11 to the left side of the basket unit. Sew the unit from step 13 to the bottom of the basket unit to make a block that measures 6½" square, including seam allowances.

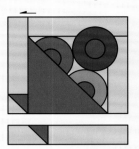 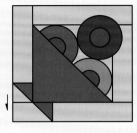

Penny Basket block

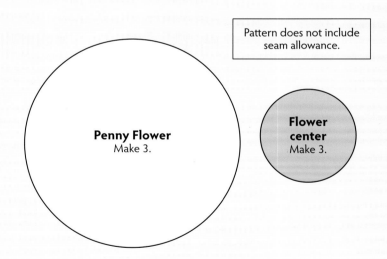

Pattern does not include
seam allowance.

Penny Flower
Make 3.

Flower center
Make 3.

08 SQUARE IN A SQUARE

by Betsy Chutchian

MATERIALS

The featured block uses 1 light and 2 dark prints.

A: 1 square, 2" × 2", of dark print #1

B: 2 squares, 2⅛" × 2⅛", of light print; cut in half diagonally to yield 4 triangles

C: 2 squares, 2½" × 2½", of dark print #2; cut in half diagonally to yield 4 triangles

D: 2 squares, 3⅛" × 3⅛", of light print; cut in half diagonally to yield 4 triangles

E: 2 squares, 4" × 4", of dark print #1; cut in half diagonally to yield 4 triangles

BLOCK ASSEMBLY

Press all seam allowances in the directions indicated by the arrows.

1. Fold the A square in half vertically and horizontally, and lightly crease to mark the center of each side. Fold the B triangles in half, and lightly crease to mark the center of the long side. Sew triangles to opposite sides of the square, matching the center creases. Sew triangles to the remaining sides of the square. Square up the unit to measure 2⅝" square, including seam allowances.

Make 1 unit.

2. Fold the C triangles in half and lightly crease to mark the center of the long side. Sew triangles to opposite sides of the unit from step 1, matching the center creases to the crossed seam. Sew triangles to the remaining sides of the square. Square up the unit to measure 3½" square, including seam allowances.

  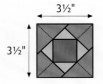

Make 1 unit.

3. Repeat step 2 using the D triangles. Square up the unit to measure 4¾" square, including seam allowances. Repeat step 2 using the E triangles to make a block. Trim the block to measure 6½" square, including seam allowances.

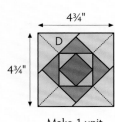

Make 1 unit.

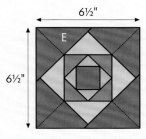

Square in a Square block

09 BASKET AND FLOWER

by Jan Patek

MATERIALS

The featured block uses 1 dark, 1 medium, and 2 light prints.

1 rectangle, 3" × 4½", of light print #1 for
    basket handle
1 rectangle, 1¾" × 2½", of light print #2 for
    flower head
3 rectangles, 1¼" × 2¼", of medium print for leaves
1 rectangle, 2¾" × 4½", of medium print for
    flower stem
1 rectangle, 3½" × 5", of light print #1 for basket
1 square, 7" × 7", of dark print for background
Freezer paper
Appliqué glue (optional)

BLOCK ASSEMBLY

The instructions are written for needle-turn appliqué, which Jan used, but use your favorite method if you prefer. All the appliqué patterns are on page 31. Reverse the patterns for fusible appliqué.

1. Trace the basket handle, flower head, leaves, flower stem, and basket onto the dull side of the freezer paper. Cut out the templates directly on the line.

2. Place each freezer-paper template on the right side of the appropriate fabric, shiny side down. Press in place.

3. Trace around the templates. Cut out the fabric shapes, adding ¼" seam allowance all around. Remove the freezer-paper template.

4. Fold the background square in half in both directions and finger-press to crease.

5. Using the creases as placement guidelines, pin, baste, or glue the pieces to the background, starting with the basket handle. Appliqué in place. Add the flower head, leaves, flower stem, and then the basket.

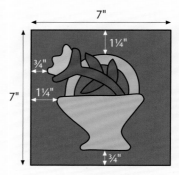

Appliqué placement guide

6. Press the block on the wrong side and trim it to 6½" square, keeping the design centered.

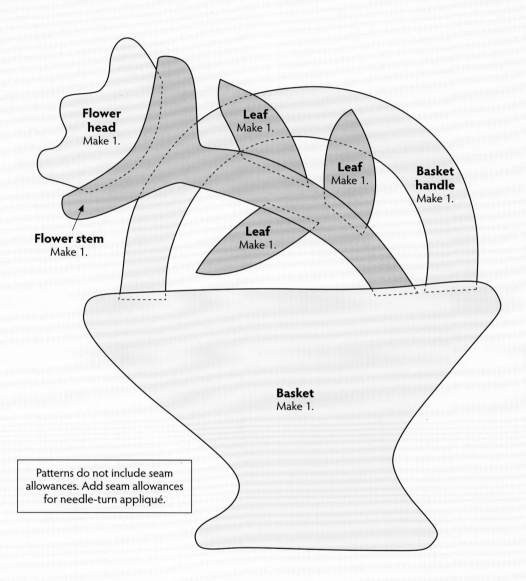

Flower head
Make 1.

Leaf
Make 1.

Leaf
Make 1.

Basket handle
Make 1.

Flower stem
Make 1.

Leaf
Make 1.

Basket
Make 1.

Patterns do not include seam allowances. Add seam allowances for needle-turn appliqué.

10 LISA'S STAR
by Lisa Bongean

MATERIALS

The featured block uses 1 light and 2 dark prints.

A: 6 squares, 1⅝" × 1⅝", of light print

B: 4 squares, 1⅝" × 1⅝", of dark print #1

C: 2 squares, 1⅝" × 1⅝", of dark print #2

D: 8 squares, 1⅝" × 1⅝", of dark print #1; cut in half diagonally to yield 16 triangles

E: 4 squares, 1⅝" × 1⅝", of dark print #2; cut in half diagonally to yield 8 triangles

F: 2 squares, 2⅜" × 2⅜", of light print; cut in half diagonally to yield 4 triangles

G: 1 square, 4¼" × 4¼", of light print; cut into quarters diagonally to yield 4 triangles

H: 4 squares, 2" × 2", of light print

BLOCK ASSEMBLY

Press all seam allowances in the directions indicated by the arrows.

1. Draw a diagonal line from corner to corner on the wrong side of each A square. Place a marked square right sides together with a B square. Sew ¼" from both sides of the drawn line. Cut the unit apart on the marked line to make two half-square-triangle units. Make eight units that measure 1¼" square, including seam allowances.

Make 8 units,
1¼" × 1¼".

2. Repeat step 1 using the remaining marked A squares and the C squares to make four half-square-triangle units that measure 1¼" square, including seam allowances.

Make 4 units,
1¼" × 1¼".

3. Join two D triangles and one A/B unit as shown. Make eight pieced triangle units.

Make 8 units.

4. Join two E triangles and one A/C unit as shown. Make four pieced triangle units.

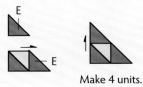

Make 4 units.

5. Join one unit from step 3 and one F triangle as shown. Make four units that measure 2" square, including seam allowances.

Make 4 units, 2" × 2".

6. Lay out the units from step 5, rotating them as shown. Sew the units together into rows. Join the rows to make the center unit, which should measure 3½" square, including seam allowances.

Make 1 unit, 3½" × 3½".

7. Sew a unit from step 3 and a unit from step 4 to the short sides of a G triangle to make a side unit. Make four units that measure 2" × 3½", including seam allowances.

Make 4 units, 2" × 3½".

8. Lay out the H squares, side units, and center unit in three rows, rotating the units as shown. Sew the units and squares together into rows. Join the rows to make a block that measures 6½" square, including seam allowances.

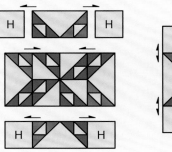
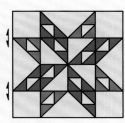

Lisa's Star block

TINY TRIANGLES

I admit, those are tiny little triangles. But they are so worth the effort! My secret is to use starch and Primitive Gatherings ¾" triangle paper. After starching my fabrics and letting them dry, I cut and then sew precisely with the help of paper foundations. You can visit www.LisaBongean.com for details. ◆

11 PUZZLED

by Carrie Nelson

MATERIALS

The featured block uses 1 light, 1 medium, and 2 dark prints.

A: 4 squares, 2⅜" × 2⅜", of light print
B: 2 squares, 2⅜" × 2⅜", of dark print #1
C: 2 squares, 2⅜" × 2⅜", of medium print
D: 4 squares, 2" × 2", of light print
E: 4 rectangles, 2" × 3½", of dark print #1
F: 4 squares, 2" × 2", of dark print #2

BLOCK ASSEMBLY

Press all seam allowances in the directions indicated by the arrows.

1. Draw a diagonal line from corner to corner on the wrong side of each A square. Place a marked square right sides together with a B square. Sew ¼" from both sides of the drawn line. Cut the unit apart on the marked line to make two half-square-triangle units. Make four units that measure 2" square, including seam allowances.

Make 4 units,
2" × 2".

2. Repeat step 1 using the remaining marked A squares and the C squares to make four half-square-triangle units that measure 2" square, including seam allowances.

Make 4 units,
2" × 2".

3. Join an A/B and A/C unit to make a two-patch unit. Make four units that measure 2" × 3½", including seam allowances.

Make 4 units,
2" × 3½".

4. Layer a D square on one end of an E rectangle, right sides together and raw edges aligned. Stitch diagonally across the D square. (You can draw a line diagonally from corner to corner or just eyeball it.) Trim the seam allowances to ¼"; press. Layer an F square on the opposite end of the E rectangle. Sew, trim, and press as shown. Make four units that measure 2" × 3½", including seam allowances.

Make 4 units,
2" × 3½".

5. Sew a unit from step 3 to a unit from step 4 to make a quarter-block unit. Make four units that measure 3½" square, including seam allowances.

Make 4 units,
3½" × 3½".

6. Lay out the units in two rows, rotating them as shown. Sew the units together into rows. Join the rows to make a block that measures 6½" square, including seam allowances.

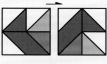
 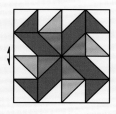

Puzzled block

ALTERNATE COLORWAYS

I've made this block a few times over the years and every time I do, I think I need to make a whole quilt with just this block. I love that changing the value and fabric placement can completely change the look of the block. ◆

12 OHIO STAR VARIATION

by Jo Morton

MATERIALS

The featured block uses 2 light, 1 medium, and 3 dark prints.

A: 4 squares, 1½" × 1½", of dark print #1
B: 8 squares, 1½" × 1½", of light print #1
C: 4 squares, 1½" × 1½", of medium print
D: 2 squares, 3¼" × 3¼", of light print #2
E: 2 squares, 3¼" × 3¼", of dark print #2
F: 1 square, 2½" × 2½", of dark print #3

BLOCK ASSEMBLY

Press all seam allowances in the directions indicated by the arrows.

1. Lay out one A, two B, and one C square in a four-patch arrangement. Sew the squares together into rows. Join the rows to make a four-patch unit. Make four units that measure 2½" square, including seam allowances.

Make 4 units,
2½" × 2½".

2. Draw a line from corner to corner on the wrong side of each D square. Place a marked square right sides together with an E square. Sew ¼" from both sides of the line. Cut on the line to make two half-square-triangle units. Make four units, 2⅞" square, including seam allowances.

Make 4 units,
2⅞" × 2⅞".

3. On the wrong side of two D/E units, draw a diagonal line from corner to corner, perpendicular to the seamline. Layer a marked unit on an unmarked D/E unit, right sides together with the dark triangles on top of the light triangles. Sew ¼" from both sides of the drawn line. Cut on the line to yield two hourglass units. Make four units that measure 2½" square, including seam allowances.

Make 4 units,
2½" × 2½".

4. Lay out the four-patch units, hourglass units, and F square in three rows, rotating the units as shown. Sew the units and square together into rows. Join the rows to make a block that measures 6½" square, including seam allowances.

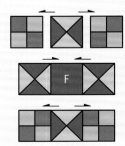 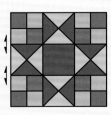

Ohio Star Variation block

13 BOW TIE QUARTET

by Lynne Hagmeier

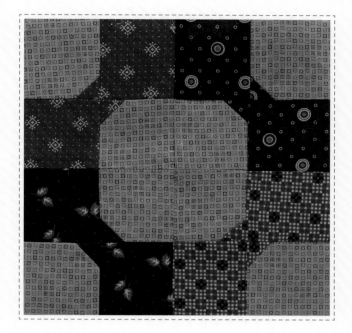

MATERIALS

The featured block uses 1 light and 4 assorted dark prints.

A: 8 squares, 1" × 1", of assorted dark prints*
B: 8 squares, 2" × 2", of light print
C: 8 squares, 2" × 2", of assorted dark prints*

*Cut in matching sets of 2 A squares and 2 C squares, all from the same print.

BLOCK ASSEMBLY

Press all seam allowances in the directions indicated by the arrows.

1. Layer an A square on one corner of a B square, right sides together and raw edges aligned. Stitch diagonally across the A square. (You can draw a line diagonally from corner to corner or just eyeball it.) Trim the seam allowances to ¼"; press. Make four sets of two matching units (8 total). Each unit should measure 2" square, including seam allowances.

Make 8 units,
2" × 2".

2. Lay out two matching units from step 1 and two C squares in two rows, rotating the units as shown. The C squares should be the same dark print as the units from step 1. Sew the units and

squares together into rows. Join the rows to make a quarter-block unit. Make four units that measure 3½" square, including seam allowances.

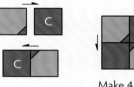

Make 4 units,
3½" × 3½".

3. Lay out the units in two rows, rotating them as shown. Sew the units together into rows. Join the rows to make a block that measures 6½" square, including seam allowances.

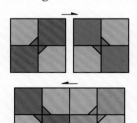 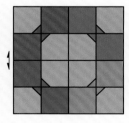

Bow Tie Quartet block

14 LAWYER'S PUZZLE

by Betsy Chutchian

MATERIALS

The featured block uses 2 light and 12 assorted dark prints.

A: 1 square, 3⅛" × 3⅛", of light print #1
B: 3 squares, 3⅛" × 3⅛", of assorted dark prints
C: 12 squares, 1⅝" × 1⅝", of light print #2
D: 12 squares, 1⅝" × 1⅝", of assorted dark prints
E: 4 squares, 1¼" × 1¼", of light print #2

BLOCK ASSEMBLY

Press all seam allowances in the directions indicated by the arrows.

1. Draw a diagonal line from corner to corner on the wrong side of the A square. Place the marked square right sides together with a B square. Sew ¼" from both sides of the drawn line. Cut the unit apart on the marked line to make two half-square-triangle units. The units should measure 2¾" square, including seam allowances.

Make 2 units,
2¾" × 2¾".

2. Repeat step 1 using the two remaining B squares to make two half-square-triangle units that measure 2¾" square, including seam allowances.

Make 2 units,
2¾" × 2¾".

3. Draw a diagonal line from corner to corner on the wrong side of each C square. Place a marked square right sides together with a D square. Sew ¼" from both sides of the drawn line. Cut the unit apart on the marked line to make two half-square-triangle units. Make 24 units that measure 1¼" square, including seam allowances.

Make 24 units,
1¼" × 1¼".

4. Sew together three units from step 3, making sure to orient them as shown. Make four strip units that measure 1¼" × 2¾", including seam allowances.

Make 4 units,
1¼" × 2¾".

Moda Blockheads

5. Sew together three units from step 3 and one E square, making sure to orient the units as shown. Make four strip units that measure 1¼" × 3½", including seam allowances.

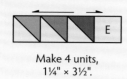

Make 4 units,
1¼" × 3½".

6. Lay out one unit from step 4, one unit from step 5, and one A/B half-square-triangle unit. Join the units to make a quarter-block unit. Make two units. Repeat to join one unit from step 4, one unit from step 5, and one B/B half-square-triangle unit to make a quarter-block unit. Make two units. The units should measure 3½" square, including seam allowances.

Make 2 of each unit,
3½" × 3½".

7. Lay out the units in two rows, rotating them as shown. Sew the units together into rows. Join the rows to make a block that measures 6½" square, including seam allowances.

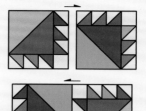 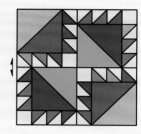

Lawyer's Puzzle block

15 FLAGS

by Jan Patek

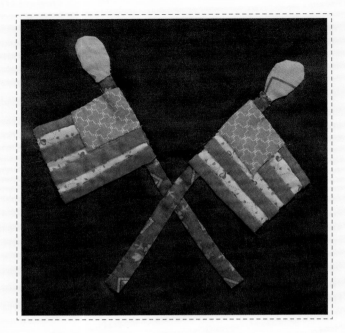

MATERIALS

The featured block uses 2 light, 2 medium, and 2 dark prints.

2 rectangles, 1" × 5½", of dark print #1 for flagpoles

2 squares, 1½" × 1½", of light print #1 for flagpole finials

2 rectangles, 2¼" × 2¾", of light print #2 for flag backgrounds

4 rectangles, 1" × 1½", of medium print #1 for short flag stripes

4 rectangles, 1" × 2½", of medium print #1 for long flag stripes

2 rectangles, 1½" × 2", of medium print #2 for flag corners

1 square, 7" × 7", of dark print #2 for background

Freezer paper

Appliqué glue (optional)

BLOCK ASSEMBLY

The instructions are written for needle-turn appliqué, which Jan used, but use your favorite method if you prefer. All the appliqué patterns are on page 41. Reverse the patterns for fusible appliqué.

1. Trace the flagpoles, finials, flag backgrounds, short stripes, long stripes, and flag corners onto the dull side of the freezer paper. Cut out the templates directly on the line.

2. Place each freezer-paper template on the right side of the appropriate fabric, shiny side down. Press in place.

3. Trace around the templates. Cut out the fabric shapes, adding ¼" seam allowance all around. Remove the freezer-paper template.

4. Fold the background square in half in both directions and finger-press to crease.

5. Using the creases as placement guidelines, pin, baste, or glue the appliqué pieces to the background, starting with the flagpoles. Appliqué in place. Add the finials, flag backgrounds, short stripes, long stripes, and then the flag corners.

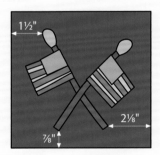

Appliqué placement diagram

6. Press the block on the wrong side and trim it to 6½" square, keeping the design centered.

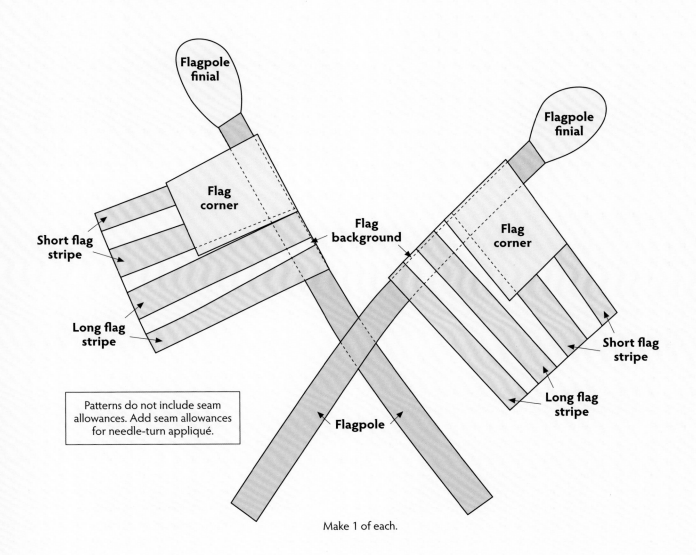

Flagpole finial

Flagpole finial

Flag corner

Flag corner

Short flag stripe

Short flag stripe

Long flag stripe

Long flag stripe

Flag background

Flagpole

Patterns do not include seam allowances. Add seam allowances for needle-turn appliqué.

Make 1 of each.

16 T BLOCK
by Jo Morton

MATERIALS

The featured block uses 1 light and 2 dark prints.

A: 2 squares, 2⅞" × 2⅞", of light print
B: 1 square, 2⅞" × 2⅞", of dark print #1
C: 1 square, 2⅞" × 2⅞", of dark print #2
D: 10 squares, 1½" × 1½", of dark print #1
E: 8 rectangles, 1½" × 2½", of light print
F: 10 squares, 1½" × 1½", of dark print #2
G: 1 square, 2½" × 2½", of light print

BLOCK ASSEMBLY

Press all seam allowances in the directions indicated by the arrows.

1. Draw a diagonal line from corner to corner on the wrong side of each A square. Place a marked square right sides together with the B square. Sew ¼" from both sides of the drawn line. Cut the unit apart on the marked line to make two half-square-triangle units. Make two units using the remaining marked A square and the C square. The units should measure 2½" square, including seam allowances.

Make 2 of each unit,
2½" × 2½".

2. Mark a diagonal line from corner to corner on the wrong side of each D and F square. Place a marked D square on one end of an E rectangle, right sides together, and stitch on the drawn line. Trim the seam allowances to ¼"; press. Place a marked F square on the opposite end of the rectangle, right sides together; stitch, trim, and press to make a flying-geese unit. Make four units and four reversed units that measure 1½" × 2½", including seam allowances.

Make 4 of each unit,
1½" × 2½".

3. Sew two matching flying-geese units together as shown to make a side unit. Make two units and two reversed units that measure 2½" square, including seam allowances.

Make 2 of each unit,
2½" × 2½".

4. Place the remaining marked D squares from step 2 on opposite corners of the G square, right sides together, and stitch on the drawn lines. Trim the seam allowances to ¼"; press. Place the remaining marked F squares on the remaining corners of the square, right sides together; stitch, trim, and press to make the center unit. The unit should measure 2½" square, including seam allowances.

Make 1 unit,
2½" × 2½".

5. Refer to the photo for placement guidance as needed. Lay out the units in three rows, rotating them as shown. Sew the units together into rows. Join the rows to make a block that measures 6½" square, including seam allowances.

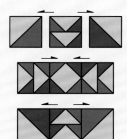 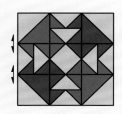

T block

"

Around the Block

"Jo Morton shared one of my favorite blocks, the T block. Why is it my favorite? It's got flying geese and half-square triangles! It's also a block that allows for a lot of variation just by changing color and value placement."

~ Carrie Nelson

17 TRAIL OF TEARS

by Lisa Bongean

MATERIALS

The featured block uses 1 light, 7 assorted medium, and 8 assorted dark prints.

A: 15 squares, 2⅜" × 2⅜", of light print
B: 8 squares, 2⅜" × 2⅜", of assorted dark prints
C: 7 squares, 2⅜" × 2⅜", of assorted medium prints*

Lisa used 1 medium print twice.

BLOCK ASSEMBLY

Press all seam allowances in the directions indicated by the arrows.

1. Draw a diagonal line from corner to corner on the wrong side of each A square. Place a marked square right sides together with a B square. Sew ¼" from both sides of the drawn line. Cut the unit apart on the marked line to make two half-square-triangle units. Make 16 units that measure 2" square, including seam allowances. You'll have 8 units left over for another project.

Make 8 units,
2" × 2".

2. Repeat step 1 using the remaining marked A squares and the C squares to make 14 half-square-triangle units that measure 2" square, including seam allowances. You'll have 6 units left over for another project.

Make 8 units,
2" × 2".

3. Lay out the half-square-triangle units in four rows, alternating and rotating them as shown. Sew the units together into rows. Join the rows to make a block that measures 6½" square, including seam allowances.

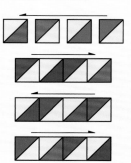 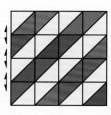

Trail of Tears block

18 CORN NO BEANS

by Carrie Nelson

MATERIALS

The featured block uses 1 light, 1 medium, and 18 assorted dark prints.

A: 14 squares, 1⅞" × 1⅞", of light print
B: 18 squares, 1⅞" × 1⅞", of assorted dark prints
C: 4 squares, 1⅞" × 1⅞", of medium print

BLOCK ASSEMBLY

Press all seam allowances in the directions indicated by the arrows.

1. Draw a diagonal line from corner to corner on the wrong side of each A square. Place a marked square right sides together with a B square. Sew ¼" from both sides of the drawn line. Cut the unit apart on the marked line to make two half-square-triangle units. Make 28 half-square-triangle units that measure 1½" square, including seam allowances.

Make 28 units,
1½" × 1½".

2. Draw a diagonal line from corner to corner on the wrong side of each C square. Repeat step 1 using the marked C squares and the remaining B squares to make eight half-square-triangle units that measure 1½" square, including seam allowances.

Make 8 units,
1½" × 1½".

3. Lay out seven A/B units and two B/C units in three rows of three units each, making sure to orient the units as shown. Sew the units together into rows. Join the rows to make a quarter-block unit. Make two of each unit. The units should measure 3½" square, including seam allowances.

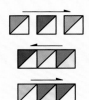

Make 2 of each unit,
3½" × 3½".

4. Lay out the units in two rows, rotating them as shown. Sew the units together into rows. Join the rows to make a block that measures 6½" square, including seam allowances.

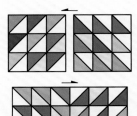 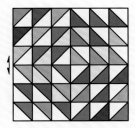

Corn No Beans block

45

Quilt Blocks

18 DEVIL'S CLAW

by Betsy Chutchian

MATERIALS

The featured block uses 1 light and 2 dark prints.

A: 2 squares, 4¼" × 4¼", of light print; cut into quarters diagonally to yield 8 triangles (2 will be extra)

B: 2 squares, 4¼" × 4¼", of dark print #1; cut into quarters diagonally to yield 8 triangles (2 will be extra)

C: 2 squares, 2⅜" × 2⅜", of dark print #2; cut in half diagonally to yield 4 triangles

D: 2 squares, 2⅜" × 2⅜", of light print; cut in half diagonally to yield 4 triangles

BLOCK ASSEMBLY

Press all seam allowances in the directions indicated by the arrows.

1. Join two A and two B triangles as shown to make the center unit. The unit should measure 3½" square, including seam allowances.

Make 1 unit,
3½" × 3½".

2. Join two C triangles and one A triangle as shown to make a flying-geese unit. Make two units that measure 2" × 3½", including seam allowances.

Make 2 units,
2" × 3½".

3. Join one A, two B, and two D triangles as shown to make a side unit. Make two units that measure 2" × 6½", including seam allowances.

Make 2 units,
2" × 6½".

4. Lay out the side units, flying-geese units, and center unit as shown. Join the flying-geese and center unit to make the center column. Sew the side units to the center column to make a block that measures 6½" square, including seam allowances.

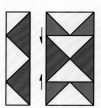

Devil's Claw block

20 NIGHT FLIGHT

by Lynne Hagmeier

MATERIALS

The featured block uses 1 light and 8 assorted dark prints.

A: 16 squares, 2" × 2", of light print
B: 8 rectangles, 2" × 3½", of assorted dark prints

BLOCK ASSEMBLY

Press all seam allowances in the directions indicated by the arrows.

1. Mark a diagonal line from corner to corner on the wrong side of each A square. Place a marked square on one end of a B rectangle, right sides together, and stitch on the drawn line. Trim the seam allowances to ¼"; press. Place a second marked square on the opposite end of the rectangle, right sides together; stitch, trim, and press to make a flying-geese unit. Make eight units that measure 2" × 3½", including seam allowances.

Make 8 units,
2" × 3½".

EASY FLYING GEESE

I hear from a lot of quilters that they avoid flying geese because they lose the points or they don't turn out square. Try stitching just to the outside (toward the corner) of your diagonally drawn line. The square will press toward the corner more accurately. ◆

2. Lay out the flying-geese units in two columns, rotating the units in one column as shown. Sew the units in each column together. Join the columns to make a block that measures 6½" square, including seam allowances.

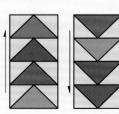 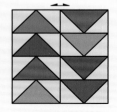

Night Flight block

21 FLYING GEESE VARIATION

by Jo Morton

MATERIALS

The featured block uses 2 light, 1 medium, and 3 dark prints.

A: 16 squares, 1½" × 1½", of light print #1
B: 4 rectangles, 1½" × 2½", of dark print #1
C: 4 rectangles, 1½" × 2½", of dark print #2
D: 4 squares, 1½" × 1½", of dark print #3
E: 1 square, 2½" × 2½", of light print #2
F: 4 squares, 2½" × 2½", of medium print

BLOCK ASSEMBLY

Press all seam allowances in the directions indicated by the arrows.

1. Mark a diagonal line from corner to corner on the wrong side of each A square. Place a marked square on one end of a B rectangle, right sides together, and stitch on the drawn line. Trim the seam allowances to ¼"; press. Place a second marked square on the opposite end of the rectangle, right sides together; stitch, trim, and press to make a flying-geese unit. Make four flying-geese units that measure 1½" × 2½", including seam allowances.

Make 4 units,
1½" × 2½".

2. Repeat step 1 using the remaining marked A squares and the C rectangles to make four flying-geese units that measure 1½" × 2½", including seam allowances.

Make 4 units,
1½" × 2½".

3. Join one A/B unit from step 1 and one A/C unit from step 2 as shown to make a side unit. Make four units that measure 2½" square, including seam allowances.

Make 4 units,
2½" × 2½".

4. Mark a diagonal line from corner to corner on the wrong side of the D squares. Place marked squares on opposite corners of the E square, right sides together, and stitch on the drawn lines. Trim the seam allowances to ¼"; press. Place marked squares on the remaining corners of the square, right sides together; stitch, trim, and press to make the center unit. The unit should measure 2½" square, including seam allowances.

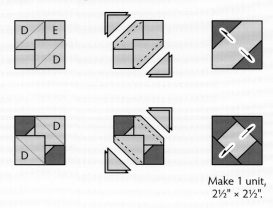

Make 1 unit,
2½" × 2½".

5. Lay out the F squares, side units, and center unit in three rows, rotating the side units as shown. Sew the units and squares together into rows. Join the rows to make a block that measures 6½" square, including seam allowances.

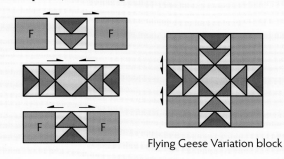

Flying Geese Variation block

> ## Around the Block
>
> *"I love making flying geese! If you have trouble getting all the pieces to align, square up the units before joining them. I enjoyed making this block and used a 1" × 2" Bloc Loc flying-geese ruler to trim the geese to a perfect 1½" × 2½" unit."*
>
> ~ BETSY CHUTCHIAN

22 ROCKY MOUNTAIN PUZZLE

by Carrie Nelson

MATERIALS

The featured block uses 1 light, 1 medium, and 2 dark prints.

A: 1 square, 2" × 2", of light print
B: 1 rectangle, 1¼" × 2", of medium print
C: 2 rectangles, 1¼" × 2¾", of medium print
D: 1 rectangle, 1¼" × 3½", of medium print
E: 6 squares, 2⅜" × 2⅜", of light print
F: 3 squares, 2⅜" × 2⅜", of dark print #1
G: 3 squares, 2⅜" × 2⅜", of dark print #2
H: 2 squares, 2" × 2", of light print

BLOCK ASSEMBLY

Press all seam allowances in the directions indicated by the arrows.

1. Sew the B rectangle to the left side of the A square. Sew C rectangles to the top and then the right side of the square. Add the D rectangle to make the center unit. The unit should measure 3½" square, including seam allowances.

Make 1 unit,
3½" × 3½".

2. Draw a diagonal line from corner to corner on the wrong side of each E square. Place a marked square right sides together with an F square. Sew ¼" from both sides of the drawn line. Cut the unit apart on the marked line to make two half-square-triangle units. Make six units that measure 2" square, including seam allowances.

Make 6 units,
2" × 2".

3. Repeat step 2 using the remaining marked E squares and the G squares to make six half-square-triangle units that measure 2" square, including seam allowances.

Make 6 units,
2" × 2".

4. Join two E/F units to make the left side unit. Join two E/G units to make the right side unit. The units should measure 2" × 3½", including seam allowances.

Make 1 of each unit,
2" × 3½".

5. Join three E/F units and one H square to make the top unit. Join three E/G units and the other H square to make the bottom unit. The units should measure 2" × 6½", including seam allowances. You'll have one E/F and one E/G unit left over for another project.

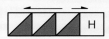 

Make 1 of each unit,
2" × 6½".

6. Lay out the center unit and the units from steps 4 and 5 in three rows, rotating them as shown. Sew the units in the center together. Join the rows to make a block that measures 6½" square, including seam allowances.

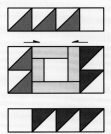 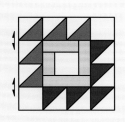

Rocky Mountain Puzzle block

23 BIRDHOUSE

by Jan Patek

MATERIALS

The featured block uses 1 light, 2 dark, and 4 medium prints.

1 rectangle, 1¼" × 2", of medium print #1 for pole

1 rectangle, 1¼" × 5", of medium print #1 for stand

1 square, 3½" × 3½", of medium print #2 for birdhouse

1 rectangle, 2" × 4", of light print for roof

2 squares, 1" × 1", of dark print #1 for doorways

1 rectangle, 2" × 4½", of medium print #3 for bird

1 rectangle, 1¼" × 1¾", of medium print #4 for bird wing

1 square, 7" × 7", of dark print #2 for background

Embroidery floss

Freezer paper

Appliqué glue (optional)

BLOCK ASSEMBLY

The instructions are written for needle-turn appliqué, which Jan used, but use your favorite method if you prefer. All the appliqué patterns are on page 53. Reverse the patterns for fusible appliqué.

1. Trace the pole, stand, birdhouse, roof, doorways, bird, and bird wing onto the dull side of the freezer paper. Cut out the templates directly on the line.

2. Place each freezer-paper template on the right side of the appropriate fabric, shiny side down. Press in place.

3. Trace around the templates. Cut out the fabric shapes, adding ¼" seam allowance all around. Remove the freezer-paper template.

4. Fold the background square in half in both directions and finger-press to crease.

5. Using the creases as placement guidelines, pin, baste, or glue the pieces to the background, starting with the pole. Appliqué in place. Add the stand, birdhouse, roof, doorways, bird, and then the wing.

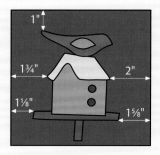

Appliqué placement guide

6. Embroider the bird's eye using two strands of embroidery floss and a stem stitch (see page 20).

7. Press the block on the wrong side and trim it to 6½" square, keeping the design centered.

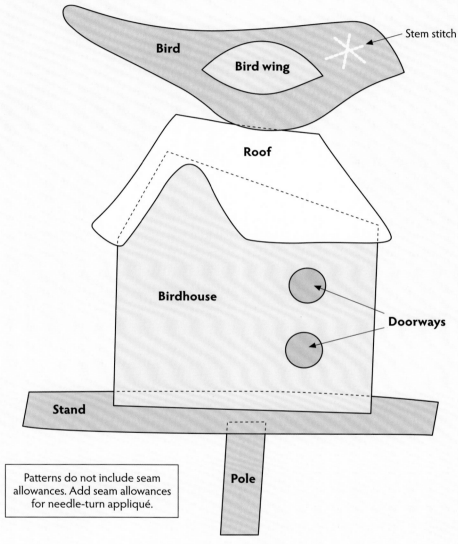

Stem stitch

Bird

Bird wing

Roof

Birdhouse

Doorways

Stand

Patterns do not include seam allowances. Add seam allowances for needle-turn appliqué.

Pole

Make 1 of each.

24 WINNECONNE STAR

by Lisa Bongean

MATERIALS

The featured block uses 1 light, 1 dark, and 8 assorted medium prints.

A: 16 squares, 1¼" × 1¼", of light print

B: 16 squares, 1¼" × 1¼", of assorted medium prints*

C: 8 squares, 2" × 2", of dark print

D: 4 rectangles, 2" × 3½", of light print

Lisa cut 2 squares from each medium print.

BLOCK ASSEMBLY

Press all seam allowances in the directions indicated by the arrows.

1. Join an A and a B square to make a two-patch unit. Make 16 units that measure 1¼" × 2", including seam allowances.

Make 16 units,
1¼" × 2".

2. Lay out eight A/B units in four rows of two units each. Sew the units together into rows. Join the rows to make the center unit, which should measure 3½" square, including seam allowances.

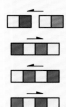

Make 1 unit,
3½" × 3½".

3. Join two A/B units as shown to make a four-patch unit. Make four units that measure 2" square, including seam allowances.

Make 4 units,
2" × 2".

4. Mark a diagonal line from corner to corner on the wrong side of each C square. Place a marked square on one end of a D rectangle, right sides together, and stitch on the drawn line. Trim the seam allowances to ¼"; press. Place a second marked square on the opposite end of the rectangle, right sides together; stitch, trim, and press to make a flying-geese unit. Make four units that measure 2" × 3½", including seam allowances.

Make 4 units,
2" × 3½".

5. Lay out the four-patch units, flying-geese units, and center unit in three rows, rotating them as shown. Sew the units together into rows. Join the rows to make a block that measures 6½" square, including seam allowances.

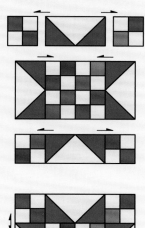

Winneconne Star block

Around the Block

"I always love red, white, and blue, and Lisa's block is just begging to be made into a small quilt for the summer holidays. Can anyone say fireworks?"

~ Lynne Hagmeier

25 TWICE THE FRIENDSHIP

by Lynne Hagmeier

MATERIALS

The featured block uses 1 light, 1 medium, and 1 dark print.

A: 2 squares, 2⅞" × 2⅞", of light print
B: 2 squares, 2⅞" × 2⅞", of medium print
C: 8 squares, 1½" × 1½", of dark print
D: 5 squares, 2½" × 2½", of light print

BLOCK ASSEMBLY

Press all seam allowances in the directions indicated by the arrows.

1. Draw a diagonal line from corner to corner on the wrong side of each A square. Place a marked square right sides together with a B square. Sew ¼" from both sides of the drawn line. Cut the unit apart on the marked line to make two half-square-triangle units. Make four units that measure 2½" square, including seam allowances.

Make 4 units,
2½" × 2½".

2. Mark a diagonal line from corner to corner on the wrong side of the C squares. Layer a marked square on one corner of a half-square-triangle unit, right sides together and raw edges aligned. Stitch on the drawn line. Trim the seam allowances to ¼". Make four side units that measure 2½" square, including seam allowances.

Make 4 units,
2½" × 2½".

3. Place marked C squares on opposite corners of a D square, right sides together, and stitch on the drawn lines. Trim the seam allowances to ¼"; press. Place marked squares on the remaining corners of the square, right sides together; stitch, trim, and press to make the center unit. Make one unit that measures 2½" square, including seam allowances.

Make 1 unit,
2½" × 2½".

4. Lay out the remaining D squares, the four side units, and the center unit in three rows, rotating the units as shown. Sew the units and squares together into rows. Join the rows to make a block that measures 6½" square, including seam allowances.

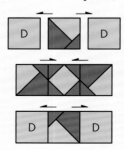 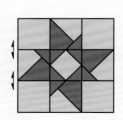

Twice the Friendship block

Layered Patchwork Twice the Friendship Block

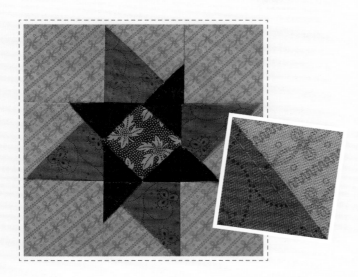

MATERIALS

The featured block uses 1 light, 1 dark, and 2 medium prints.

A: 2 squares, 2½" × 2½", of medium print #1;
    cut in half diagonally to yield 4 triangles

B: 8 squares, 2½" × 2½", of light print

C: 4 squares, 1½" × 1½", of dark print; cut in half
    diagonally to yield 8 triangles

D: 1 square, 2½" × 2½", of medium print #2
Water-soluble glue stick

BLOCK ASSEMBLY

Press all seam allowances in the directions
indicated by the arrows.

1. Glue baste an A triangle on a B square, right
sides facing up and 90° corners aligned. Using
coordinating thread, topstitch ⅛" from the bias
edge of the triangle. Make four units that measure
2½" square, including seam allowances.

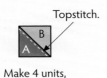

Topstitch.

Make 4 units,
2½" × 2½".

2. Glue baste a C triangle on one corner of a
half-square-triangle unit, right sides facing up
and 90° corners aligned. Using coordinating
thread, topstitch ⅛" from the bias edge of the
triangle. Make four side units that measure 2½"
square, including seam allowances.

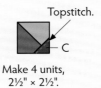

Topstitch.

C

Make 4 units,
2½" × 2½".

3. Glue baste four C triangles on the D square,
right sides facing up and 90° corners aligned.
Using coordinating thread, topstitch ⅛" from the
bias edge of each triangle. Make one center unit
that measures 2½" square, including seam
allowances.

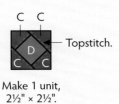

C   C

D   Topstitch.

C   C

Make 1 unit,
2½" × 2½".

4. Lay out the remaining B squares, the four
side units, and the center unit in three rows,
rotating the units as shown. Sew the units and
squares together into rows. Join the rows to
make a block that measures 6½" square, including
seam allowances.

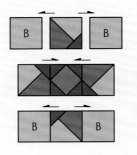

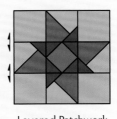

Layered Patchwork
Twice the Friendship block

26 UNION VARIATION

by Jo Morton

MATERIALS

The featured block uses 2 light, 1 medium, and 2 dark prints.

A: 1 square, 2½" × 2½", of dark print #1

B: 2 squares, 2⅜" × 2⅜", of light print #1; cut in half diagonally to yield 4 triangles

C: 2 squares, 2⅞" × 2⅞", of medium print; cut in half diagonally to yield 4 triangles

D: 6 squares, 1⅞" × 1⅞", of light print #2

E: 6 squares, 1⅞" × 1⅞", of dark print #2

F: 4 rectangles, 1½" × 2½", of light print #2

BLOCK ASSEMBLY

Press all seam allowances in the directions indicated by the arrows.

1. Fold the A square in half vertically and horizontally, and lightly crease to mark the center of each side. Fold the B triangles in half, and lightly crease to mark the center of the long side. Sew triangles to opposite sides of the square, matching the center creases; press. Sew triangles to the remaining sides of the square. Square up the unit to measure 3⅜" square, including seam allowances.

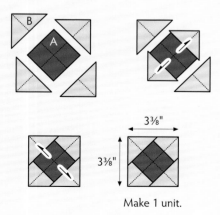

Make 1 unit.

2. Fold the C triangles in half, and lightly crease to mark the center of the long side. Sew triangles to opposite sides of the unit from step 1, matching the center creases to the crossed seam; press. Sew triangles to the remaining sides of the unit to make the center unit. Square up the unit to measure 4½" square, including seam allowances.

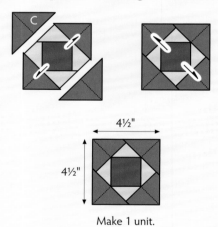

Make 1 unit.

3. Draw a diagonal line from corner to corner on the wrong side of each D square. Place a marked square right sides together with an E square. Sew ¼" from both sides of the drawn line. Cut the unit apart on the marked line to make two half-square-triangle units. Make 12 units that measure 1½" square, including seam allowances.

Make 12 units,
1½" × 1½".

MAKE TRIANGLES EASIER

These half-triangle squares finish at 1". Because there are more than a few of them and they're all the same two prints, this is a great time to use triangle paper. Do you use it? I do, and two papers that work perfectly here are Primitive Gatherings Triangle Paper and Spinning Stars Triangle Paper—both in the 1" finished size. ◆

4. Sew a half-square-triangle unit to each end of an F rectangle. Make two units that measure 1½" × 4½", including seam allowances.

Make 2 units,
1½" × 4½".

5. Sew two half-square-triangle units to each end of an F rectangle. Make two units that measure 1½" × 6½", including seam allowances.

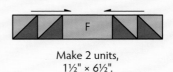

Make 2 units,
1½" × 6½".

6. Lay out the units from steps 4 and 5 and the center unit in three rows, rotating the units as shown. Sew the units in the center row together. Join the rows to make a block that measures 6½" square, including seam allowances.

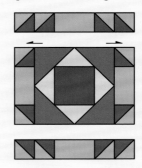 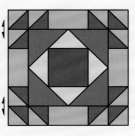

Union Variation block

27 PUMPKIN

by Jan Patek

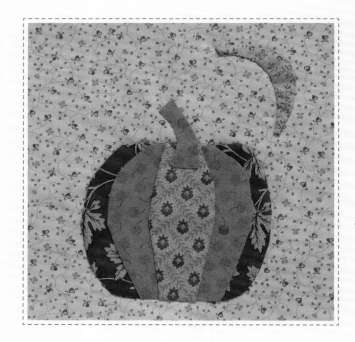

MATERIALS

The featured block uses 1 light and 4 medium prints.

1 rectangle, 4¼" × 4¾", of medium print #1 for
   pumpkin A
1 rectangle, 3¾" × 4", of medium print #2 for
   pumpkin B
1 rectangle, 2¼" × 4", of medium print #3 for
   pumpkin C
1 rectangle, 1½" × 2¼", of medium print #2 for stem
1 rectangle, 2¼" × 4", of medium print #4 for moon
1 square, 7" × 7", of light print for background
Freezer paper
Appliqué glue (optional)

BLOCK ASSEMBLY

The instructions are written for needle-turn
appliqué, which Jan used, but use your favorite
method if you prefer. All the appliqué patterns are
on page 61. Reverse the patterns for fusible
appliqué.

1. Trace pumpkin shapes A–C, the stem, and the
moon onto the dull side of the freezer paper. Cut
out the templates directly on the line.

2. Place each freezer-paper template on the right
side of the appropriate fabric, shiny side down.
Press in place.

3. Trace around the templates. Cut out the fabric
shapes, adding ¼" seam allowance all around.
Remove the freezer-paper template.

4. Fold the background square in half in both
directions and finger-press to crease.

5. Using the creases as placement guidelines,
pin, baste, or glue the pieces to the background,
starting with pumpkin A. Appliqué in place.
Add pumpkin B, pumpkin C, and then the stem.
Appliqué the moon in place.

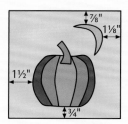

Appliqué placement guide

5. Press the block on the wrong side and trim
it to 6½" square, keeping the design centered.

APPLIQUÉ LIKE A PRO

I use Sewline marking pencils for appliqué
pieces because they make a nice sharp stitching
line. If you plan to hand quilt your project, cut
away the fabric behind the appliqués to reduce
bulk. If you're machine quilting, the bulk
shouldn't cause a problem. ◆

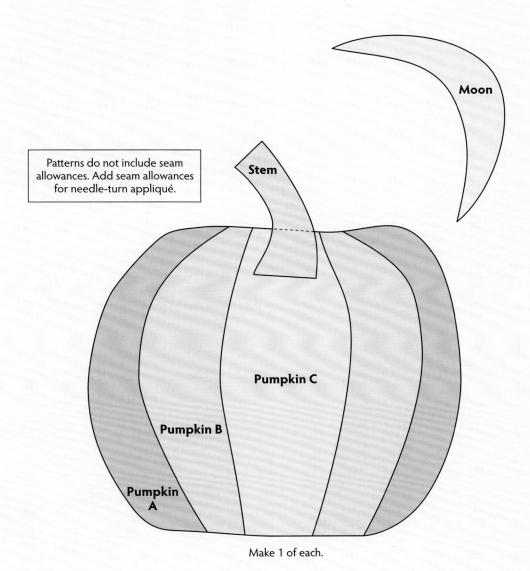

Patterns do not include seam allowances. Add seam allowances for needle-turn appliqué.

Moon

Stem

Pumpkin C

Pumpkin B

Pumpkin A

Make 1 of each.

28 JUNEAU

by Lisa Bongean

MATERIALS

The featured block uses 1 medium, 1 dark, and 2 light prints.

A: 4 squares, 2" × 2", of light print #1

B: 1 square, 3½" × 3½", of dark print

C: 2 squares, 2⅜" × 2⅜", of light print #2

D: 2 squares, 2⅜" × 2⅜", of dark print

E: 8 squares, 1¼" × 1¼", of dark print

F: 4 rectangles, 1¼" × 2", of light print #2

G: 4 squares, 1⅝" × 1⅝", of light print #2; cut in half diagonally to yield 8 triangles

H: 1 square, 2¾" × 2¾", of light print #2; cut into quarters diagonally to yield 4 triangles

I: 4 squares, 2⅜" × 2⅜", of medium print; cut in half diagonally to yield 8 triangles

STARCH MAKES THE DIFFERENCE

Have I mentioned starch? I'm often asked about working with such small pieces. If you starch your fabrics, let them dry, and then press them with or without steam before you cut and sew them, the pieces behave really well when you sew them! ◆

BLOCK ASSEMBLY

Press all seam allowances in the directions indicated by the arrows.

1. Draw a diagonal line from corner to corner on the wrong side of the A squares. Place marked squares on opposite corners of the B square, right sides together, and stitch on the drawn lines. Trim the seam allowances to ¼"; press. Place marked squares on the remaining corners of the B square, right sides together; stitch, trim, and press to make the center unit. Make one unit that measures 3½" square, including seam allowances.

Make 1 unit,
3½" × 3½".

2. Draw a diagonal line from corner to corner on the wrong side of each C square. Place a marked square right sides together with a D square. Sew ¼" from both sides of the drawn line. Cut the unit apart on the marked line to make two half-square-triangle units. Make four units that measure 2" square, including seam allowances.

Make 4 units,
2" × 2".

3. Mark a diagonal line from corner to corner on the wrong side of the E squares. Place a marked square on one end of an F rectangle, right sides together, and stitch on the drawn line. Trim the seam allowances to ¼"; press. Place a second marked square on the opposite end of the rectangle, right sides together; stitch, trim, and press to make a flying-geese unit. Make four units that measure 1¼" × 2", including seam allowances.

Make 4 units,
1¼" × 2".

4. Sew G triangles to the ends of a flying-geese unit. Press. Sew an H triangle to the bottom of the unit to make a pieced triangle unit. Make four units.

Make 4 units.

5. Sew I triangles to the sides of a triangle unit from step 4. Make four units that measure 2" × 3½", including seam allowances.

Make 4 units,
2" × 3½".

6. Lay out the pieced units in three rows, rotating them as shown. Sew the units together into rows. Join the rows to make a block that measures 6½" square, including seam allowances.

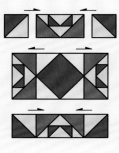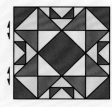

Juneau block

29 CAT'S CRADLE

by Betsy Chutchian

MATERIALS

The featured block uses 1 dark and 2 light prints.

A: 3 squares, 1⅞" × 1⅞", of light print #1

B: 3 squares, 1⅞" × 1⅞", of dark print

C: 6 squares, 1⅞" × 1⅞", of dark print; cut in half diagonally to yield 12 triangles

D: 3 squares, 2⅞" × 2⅞", of light print #2; cut in half diagonally to yield 6 triangles

E: 3 squares, 2½" × 2½", of light print #2

BLOCK ASSEMBLY

Press all seam allowances in the directions indicated by the arrows.

1. Draw a diagonal line from corner to corner on the wrong side of each A square. Place a marked square right sides together with a B square. Sew ¼" from both sides of the drawn line. Cut the unit apart on the marked line to make two half-square-triangle units. Make six units that measure 1½" square, including seam allowances.

Make 6 units,
1½" × 1½".

2. Sew C triangles to adjacent sides of a half-square-triangle unit as shown. Make six pieced triangle units.

Make 6 units.

3. Sew a D triangle to a triangle unit from step 2 as shown. Make six units that measure 2½" square, including seam allowances.

Make 6 units,
2½" × 2½".

4. Lay out the units from step 3 and the E squares in three rows, rotating the units as shown. Sew the units and squares together into rows. Join the rows to make a block that measures 6½" square, including seam allowances.

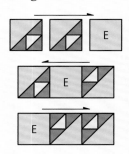 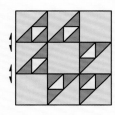

Cat's Cradle block

30 FOUR PATCH DASH

by Carrie Nelson

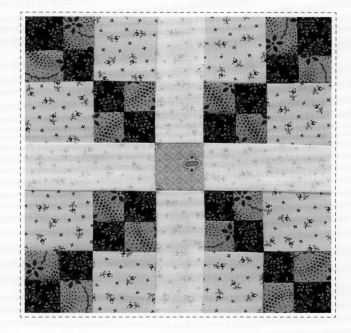

MATERIALS

The featured block uses 2 light, 1 dark, and 2 medium prints.

A: 16 squares, 1⅛" × 1⅛", of dark print
B: 16 squares, 1⅛" × 1⅛", of medium print #1
C: 8 squares, 1¾" × 1¾", of light print #1
D: 4 rectangles, 1½" × 3", of light print #2
E: 1 square, 1½" × 1½", of medium print #2

BLOCK ASSEMBLY

Press all seam allowances in the directions indicated by the arrows.

1. Join two A and two B squares as shown to make a four-patch unit. Make eight units that measure 1¾" square.

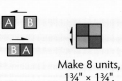

Make 8 units,
1¾" × 1¾".

2. Lay out two four-patch units and two C squares in a four-patch arrangement. Sew the units and squares together into rows. Join the rows to make a corner unit. Make four units that measure 3" square, including seam allowances.

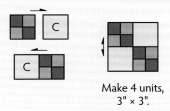

Make 4 units,
3" × 3".

3. Lay out the corner units, D rectangles, and E square in three rows, rotating the units as shown. Sew the pieces together into rows. Join the rows to make a block that measures 6½" square, including seam allowances.

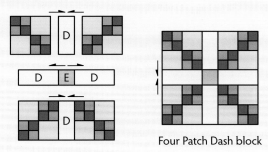

Four Patch Dash block

31 DOT DASH

by Lynne Hagmeier

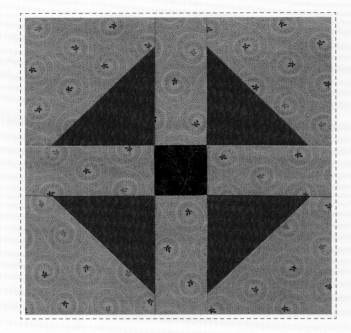

MATERIALS

The featured block uses 1 light and 2 dark prints.

A: 4 squares, 2½" × 2½", of dark print #1
B: 4 squares, 3" × 3", of light print
C: 4 rectangles, 1½" × 3", of light print
D: 1 square, 1½" × 1½", of dark print #2

FLOATING TRIANGLES

I love a simple Churn Dash block but sometimes find the points fighting each other when I sew the blocks together. Solution? Have the block triangles float within the background so the background creates its own sashing, allowing each Churn Dash to shine with perfect points. ◆

BLOCK ASSEMBLY

Press all seam allowances in the directions indicated by the arrows.

1. Draw a diagonal line from corner to corner on the wrong side of each A square. Place a marked square on one corner of a B square, right sides together, and stitch on the drawn line. Trim the seam allowances to ¼". Make four units that measure 3" square, including seam allowances.

Make 4 units,
3" × 3".

2. Lay out the A/B units, C rectangles, and D square in three rows, rotating the units as shown. Sew the pieces together into rows. Join the rows to make a block that measures 6½" square, including seam allowances.

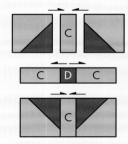 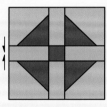

Dot Dash block

32 DUTCHMAN'S PUZZLE

by Betsy Chutchian

MATERIALS

The featured block uses 2 light and 2 dark prints.

A: 8 squares, 2" × 2", of light print #1
B: 4 rectangles, 2" × 3½", of dark print #1
C: 8 squares, 2" × 2", of light print #2
D: 4 rectangles, 2" × 3½", of dark print #2

BLOCK ASSEMBLY

Press all seam allowances in the directions indicated by the arrows.

1. Mark a line from corner to corner on the wrong side of the A squares. Place a marked square on one end of a B rectangle, right sides together, and stitch on the line. Trim the seam allowances to ¼"; press. Place a marked square on the opposite end of the rectangle, right sides together; stitch, trim, and press to make a flying-geese unit. Make four units that measure 2" × 3½".

Make 4 units,
2" × 3½".

2. Repeat step 1 using the C squares and D rectangles to make four flying-geese units that measure 2" × 3½", including seam allowances.

Make 4 units,
2" × 3½".

3. Sew an A/B unit to a C/D unit to make a quarter-block unit. Make four units that measure 3½" square, including seam allowances.

Make 4 units,
3½" × 3½".

4. Lay out the units in two rows, rotating them as shown. Sew the units together into rows. Join the rows to make a block that measures 6½" square, including seam allowances.

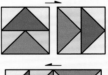 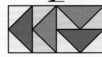 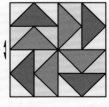

Dutchman's Puzzle block

Quilt Blocks

33 STARZ

by Jo Morton

MATERIALS

The featured block uses 3 light and 2 dark prints.

A: 4 squares, 1⅞" × 1⅞", of light print #1
B: 4 squares, 1⅞" × 1⅞", of dark print #1
C: 4 squares, 1½" × 1½", of dark print #1
D: 4 squares, 1½" × 1½", of dark print #2
E: 8 squares, 1½" × 1½", of light print #2
F: 4 rectangles, 1½" × 2½", of dark print #2
G: 4 rectangles, 1½" × 2½", of light print #3
H: 1 square, 2½" × 2½", of light print #3

BLOCK ASSEMBLY

Press all seam allowances in the directions indicated by the arrows.

1. Draw a diagonal line from corner to corner on the wrong side of each A square. Place a marked square right sides together with a B square. Sew ¼" from both sides of the drawn line. Cut the unit apart on the marked line to make two half-square-triangle units. Make eight units that measure 1½" square, including seam allowances.

Make 8 units,
1½" × 1½".

2. Lay out one C square, two half-square-triangle units, and one D square in a four-patch arrangement. Sew the pieces together into rows. Join the rows to make a corner unit. Make four units that measure 2½" square, including seam allowances.

Make 4 units,
2½" × 2½".

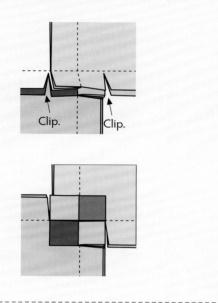

3. Mark a diagonal line from corner to corner on the wrong side of the E squares. Place a marked square on one end of an F rectangle, right sides together, and stitch on the drawn line. Trim the seam allowances to ¼"; press. Place a second marked square on the opposite end of the rectangle, right sides together; stitch, trim, and press to make a flying-geese unit. Make four units that measure 1½" × 2½", including seam allowances.

Make 4 units,
1½" × 2½".

4. Sew a G rectangle to the top of a flying-geese unit to make a side unit. Make four units that measure 2½" square, including seam allowances.

Make 4 units,
2½" × 2½".

5. Lay out the corner units, side units, and H square in three rows, rotating the units as shown. Sew the units and square together into rows. Join the rows to make a block that measures 6½" square, including seam allowances.

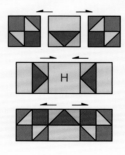 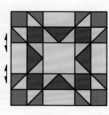

Starz block

34 HOUSE

by Jan Patek

MATERIALS

The featured block uses 2 light, 3 medium, and 2 dark prints.

1 rectangle, 2¼" × 6¾", of medium print #1
  for grass
1 rectangle, 3¾" × 4¼", of medium print #2
  for house
3 rectangles, 1¼" × 4¼", of dark print #1 for
  house logs
1 rectangle, 1¼" × 1½", of light print #1 for window
1 rectangle, 1¼" × 2", of dark print #2 for door
1 square, 1½" × 1½", of dark print #2 for chimney
1 rectangle, 2" × 4½", of dark print #2 for roof
1 rectangle, 1¾" × 3¼", of light print #2 for moon
1 square, 7" × 7", of medium print #3 for background
Freezer paper
Appliqué glue (optional)

BLOCK ASSEMBLY

The instructions are written for needle-turn appliqué, which Jan used, but use your favorite method if you prefer. All the appliqué patterns are on page 71. Reverse the patterns for fusible appliqué.

1. Trace the grass, house, house logs, window, door, chimney, roof, and moon onto the dull side of the freezer paper. Cut out the templates directly on the line.

2. Place each freezer-paper template on the right side of the appropriate fabric, shiny side down. Press in place.

3. Trace around the templates. Cut out the fabric shapes, adding ¼" seam allowance all around. Remove the freezer-paper template.

4. Pin, baste, or glue the pieces to the background, starting with the grass. Appliqué in place. Add the house, house logs, window, door, chimney, and then the roof. Appliqué the moon in place.

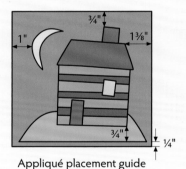

Appliqué placement guide

5. Press the block on the wrong side and trim it to 6½" square, keeping the design centered.

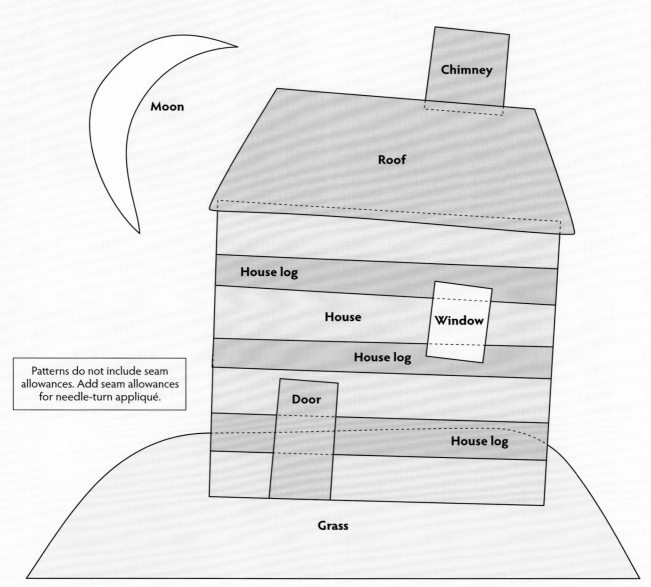

Moon

Chimney

Roof

House log

House

Window

House log

Patterns do not include seam allowances. Add seam allowances for needle-turn appliqué.

Door

House log

Grass

Make 1 of each.

Quilt Blocks

35 NORTHRIDGE

by Lisa Bongean

MATERIALS

The featured block uses 1 light and 2 dark prints.

A: 4 squares, 2" × 2", of light print

B: 1 square, 3½" × 3½", of dark print #1

C: 2 squares, 2⅜" × 2⅜", of light print

D: 2 squares, 2⅜" × 2⅜", of dark print #1

E: 3 squares, 2¾" × 2¾", of dark print #2; cut into quarters diagonally to yield 12 triangles

F: 1 square, 2¾" × 2¾", of light print; cut into quarters diagonally to yield 4 triangles

G: 4 squares, 2⅜" × 2⅜", of light print; cut in half diagonally to yield 8 triangles

---

ACCURACY COUNTS

The most important step in making blocks with tiny pieces is accurate cutting. If your cutting is off even slightly, it can make a huge impact on the success of your block. Look for rulers, like my Itty-Bitty Eights rulers from Creative Grids, where all the lines are dashed; the dashed lines enable you to see your fabric edges at all times. ◆

BLOCK ASSEMBLY

Press all seam allowances in the directions indicated by the arrows.

1. Draw a diagonal line from corner to corner on the wrong side of the A squares. Place marked squares on opposite corners of the B square, right sides together, and stitch on the drawn lines. Trim the seam allowances to ¼"; press. Place marked squares on the remaining corners of the B square, right sides together; stitch, trim, and press to make the center unit. Make one unit that measures 3½" square, including seam allowances.

Make 1 unit,
3½" × 3½".

2. Draw a diagonal line from corner to corner on the wrong side of each C square. Place a marked square right sides together with a D square. Sew ¼" from both sides of the drawn line. Cut the unit apart on the marked line to make two half-square-triangle units. Make four units that measure 2" square, including seam allowances.

Make 4 units,
2" × 2".

3. Join an E triangle and an F triangle along their long edges to make a half-square-triangle unit. Make four units that measure 1½" square, including seam allowances.

Make 4 units,
1½" × 1½".

4. Sew two E triangles to an E/F unit as shown to make a pieced triangle unit. Make four units.

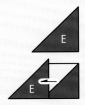

Make 4 units.

5. Sew G triangles to the short sides of a triangle unit from step 4 to make a side unit. Make four units that measure 2" × 3½", including seam allowances.

Make 4 units,
2" × 3½".

6. Lay out the half-square-triangle units from step 2, the side units, and the center unit in three rows, rotating them as shown. Sew the units together into rows. Join the rows to make a block that measures 6½" square, including seam allowances.

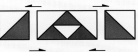

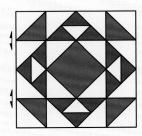

Northridge block

36 SHOO DAT

by Carrie Nelson

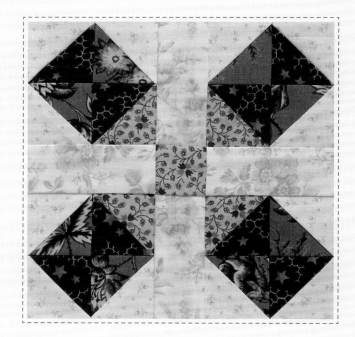

MATERIALS

The featured block uses 2 light, 1 medium, and 2 dark prints.

A: 6 squares, 2⅛" × 2⅛", of light print #1
B: 4 squares, 2⅛" × 2⅛", of dark print #1
C: 4 squares, 2⅛" × 2⅛", of dark print #2
D: 2 squares, 2⅛" × 2⅛", of medium print
E: 4 rectangles, 1½" × 3", of light print #2
F: 1 square, 1½" × 1½", of medium print

BLOCK ASSEMBLY

Press all seam allowances in the directions indicated by the arrows.

1. Draw a diagonal line from corner to corner on the wrong side of each A square. Place a marked square right sides together with a B square. Sew ¼" from both sides of the drawn line. Cut the unit apart on the marked line to make two half-square-triangle units. Make four units that measure 1¾" square, including seam allowances.

Make 4 units,
1¾" × 1¾".

2. Repeat step 1 using the remaining marked A squares and the C squares to make eight units that measure 1¾" square, including seam allowances.

Make 8 units,
1¾" × 1¾".

3. Draw a diagonal line from corner to corner on the wrong side of each D square. Place a marked square right sides together with a B square. Sew ¼" from both sides of the drawn line. Cut the unit apart on the marked line to make two half-square-triangle units. Make four units that measure 1¾" square, including seam allowances.

Make 4 units,
1¾" × 1¾".

4. Lay out one A/B unit, two A/C units, and one B/D unit in a four-patch arrangement as shown. Sew the units together into rows. Join the rows to make a corner unit. Make four units that measure 3" square, including seam allowances.

Make 4 units,
3" × 3".

5. Lay out the corner units, E rectangles, and F square in three rows, rotating the units as shown. Sew the pieces together into rows. Join the rows to make a block that measures 6½" square, including seam allowances.

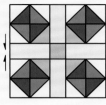

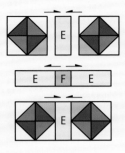

Shoo Dat block

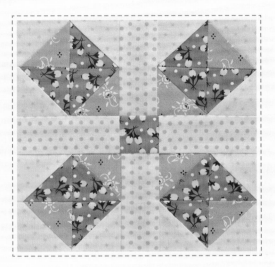

"

Around the Block

"Carrie offers us a fun, easy block that's basically four Square-in-a-Square blocks with sashing. For an even quicker version, substitute four 3" squares in place of the units from step 4. Very cool!"

~ LYNNE HAGMEIER

37 DOUBLE DELIGHT STAR

by Lynne Hagmeier

MATERIALS

The featured block uses 1 light and 2 dark prints.

A: 12 squares, 1½" × 1½", of light print
B: 8 rectangles, 1½" × 2½", of dark print #1
C: 8 squares, 1½" × 1½", of dark print #2
D: 4 rectangles, 1½" × 2½", of light print
E: 4 squares, 1½" × 1½", of dark print #1
F: 1 square, 2½" × 2½", of dark print #2

BLOCK ASSEMBLY

Press all seam allowances in the directions indicated by the arrows.

1. Mark a diagonal line from corner to corner on the wrong side of eight A squares. Place a marked square on one end of a B rectangle, right sides together, and stitch on the drawn line. Trim the seam allowances to ¼"; press. Place a second marked square on the opposite end of the rectangle, right sides together; stitch, trim, and press to make a flying-geese unit. Make four units that measure 1½" × 2½", including seam allowances.

Make 4 units,
1½" × 2½".

2. Mark a diagonal line from corner to corner on the wrong side of the C squares. Place a marked square on one end of a D rectangle, right sides together, and stitch on the drawn line. Trim the seam allowances to ¼"; press. Place a second marked square on the opposite end of the rectangle, right sides together; stitch, trim, and press to make a flying-geese unit. Make four units that measure 1½" × 2½", including seam allowances.

Make 4 units,
1½" × 2½".

3. Sew an A/B unit to a C/D unit as shown to make a side unit. Make four units that measure 2½" square, including seam allowances.

Make 4 units,
2½" × 2½".

4. Sew A and E squares together as shown to make a two-patch unit. Make four units that measure 1½" × 2½", including seam allowances.

Make 4 units,
1½" × 2½".

5. Sew a B rectangle to the top of an A/E unit to make a corner unit. Make four units that measure 2½" square, including seam allowances.

Make 4 units,
2½" × 2½".

6. Lay out the corner units, side units, and F square in three rows, rotating the units as shown. Sew the units and square together into rows. Join the rows to make a block that measures 6½" square, including seam allowances.

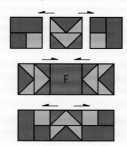 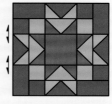

Double Delight Star block

77

Quilt Blocks

38 FRAMED STAR

by Jo Morton

MATERIALS

The featured block uses 1 light, 1 medium, and 1 dark print.

A: 24 squares, 1½" × 1½", of light print
B: 12 rectangles, 1½" × 2½", of medium print
C: 8 squares, 1½" × 1½", of dark print
D: 1 square, 2½" × 2½", of light print

BLOCK ASSEMBLY

Press all seam allowances in the directions indicated by the arrows.

1. Mark a diagonal line from corner to corner on the wrong side of the A squares. Place a marked square on one end of a B rectangle, right sides together, and stitch on the drawn line. Trim the seam allowances to ¼"; press. Place a second marked square on the opposite end of the rectangle, right sides together; stitch, trim, and press to make a flying-geese unit. Make 12 units that measure 1½" × 2½", including seam allowances.

Make 12 units,
1½" × 2½".

2. Lay out four C squares, four flying-geese units, and the D square in three rows, rotating the units as shown. Sew the units and squares together into rows. Join the rows to make the center unit. Make one unit that measures 4½" square, including seam allowances.

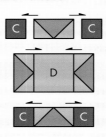

Make 1 unit,
4½" × 4½".

Moda Blockheads

3. Join two flying-geese units as shown to make a side unit. Make two units that measure 1½" × 4½", including seam allowances.

Make 2 units,
1½" × 4½".

4. Sew two C squares and two flying-geese units together as shown to make the top unit. Repeat to make the bottom unit. The units should measure 1½" × 6½", including seam allowances.

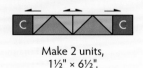

Make 2 units,
1½" × 6½".

5. Lay out the units from steps 2, 3, and 4 in three rows, rotating them as shown. Sew the units in the center row together. Join the rows to make a block that measures 6½" square, including seam allowances.

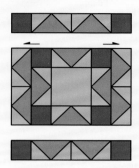
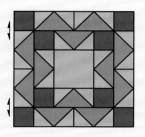

Framed Star block

❝

Around the Block

"I couldn't resist doctoring my version of this block a bit. I simply changed the 2½" D square into a Square-in-a-Square unit. (See my block in my quilt on page 12.) Start with a 2½" square, then sew a 1¼" square to each corner using the folded-corner technique.

~ CARRIE NELSON

39 CAT AND DOG

by Jan Patek

MATERIALS

The featured block uses 1 light, 1 dark, and 1 medium print.

1 rectangle, 2¾" × 4½", of light print for cat
1 rectangle, 3¼" × 4¾", of dark print for dog
1 square, 7" × 7", of medium print for background
Embroidery floss
Freezer paper
Appliqué glue (optional)

BLOCK ASSEMBLY

The instructions are written for needle-turn appliqué, which Jan used, but use your favorite method if you prefer. All the appliqué patterns are on page 81. Reverse the patterns for fusible appliqué.

1. Trace the cat and dog onto the dull side of the freezer paper. Cut out the templates directly on the line.

2. Place each freezer-paper template on the right side of the appropriate fabric, shiny side down. Press in place.

SANDPAPER BOARD TO THE RESCUE

After ironing the freezer paper shapes to the right side of your fabric, lay the fabric on a sandpaper board and trace around the pattern with a marking pencil to create a turn-under line. The fabric won't stretch out of shape as you trace! ◆

3. Trace around the templates. Cut out the fabric shapes, adding ¼" seam allowance all around. Remove the freezer-paper template.

4. Pin, baste, or glue the cat and dog to the background and appliqué in place.

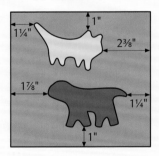

Appliqué placement diagram

5. Embroider the cat's whiskers using two strands of embroidery floss and a stem stitch (see page 20).

6. Press the block on the wrong side and trim it to 6½" square, keeping the design centered.

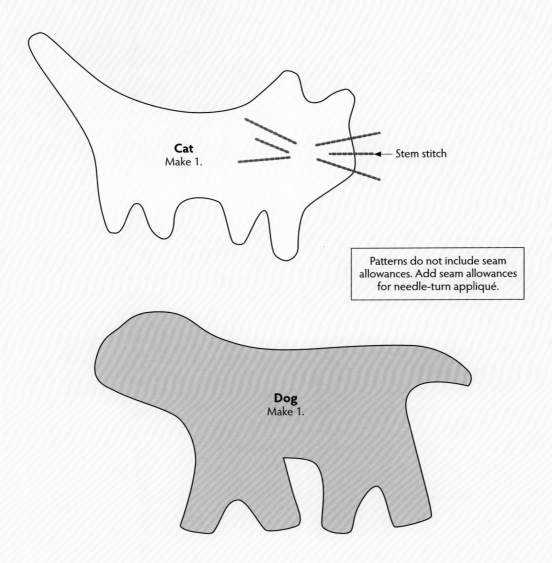

Cat
Make 1.

← Stem stitch

Patterns do not include seam
allowances. Add seam allowances
for needle-turn appliqué.

Dog
Make 1.

40 BASKET OF TRIANGLES

by Betsy Chutchian

MATERIALS

The featured block uses 2 light and 2 dark prints.

A: 5 squares, 1⅞" × 1⅞", of light print #1
B: 4 squares, 1⅞" × 1⅞", of dark print #1
C: 3 squares, 1⅞" × 1⅞", of light print #2
D: 4 squares, 1⅞" × 1⅞", of dark print #2
E: 2 squares, 1⅞" × 1⅞", of dark print #2; cut in half diagonally to yield 4 triangles
F: 1 square, 4⅞" × 4⅞", of light print #2; cut in half diagonally to yield 2 triangles (1 will be extra)
G: 2 squares, 1½" × 1½", of light print #1
H: 2 rectangles, 1½" × 4½", of light print #1

BLOCK ASSEMBLY

Press all seam allowances in the directions indicated by the arrows.

1. Draw a diagonal line from corner to corner on the wrong side of each A square. Place a marked square right sides together with a B square. Sew ¼" from both sides of the drawn line. Cut the unit apart on the marked line to make two half-square-triangle units. Make eight units that measure 1½" square, including seam allowances.

Make 8 units,
1½" × 1½".

2. Repeat step 1 using the C and D squares to make six half-square-triangle units. Use the remaining marked A square and D square to make two half-square-triangle units. The units should measure 1½" square, including seam allowances.

Make 6 units,
1½" × 1½".

Make 2 units,
1½" × 1½".

3. Lay out the C/D half-square-triangle units and the E triangles as shown. Join the pieces into rows; press. Join the rows to make a pieced triangle unit.

Make 1 unit.

4. Join the triangle unit from step 3 and one F triangle to make a basket unit that measures 4½" square, including seam allowances.

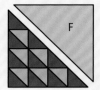

Make 1 unit,
4½" × 4½".

5. Join four A/B half-square-triangle units, making sure to orient them as shown. Make one unit that measures 1½" × 4½", including seam allowances.

Make 1 unit,
1½" × 4½".

6. Join one G square and the four remaining A/B half-square-triangle units, making sure to orient the units as shown. Make one unit that measures 1½" × 5½", including seam allowances.

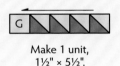

Make 1 unit,
1½" × 5½".

7. Sew the units from steps 5 and 6 to the basket unit as shown. The basket unit should now measure 5½" square, including seam allowances.

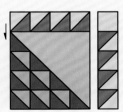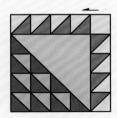

Make 1 unit,
5½" × 5½".

8. Sew an A/D half-square-triangle unit to one end of an H rectangle, making sure to orient the unit as shown. Make one unit that measures 1½" × 5½", including seam allowances.

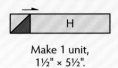

Make 1 unit,
1½" × 5½".

9. Join the remaining G square, A/D half-square-triangle unit, and H rectangle, making sure to orient the unit as shown. Make one unit that measures 1½" × 6½", including seam allowances.

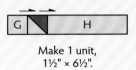

Make 1 unit,
1½" × 6½".

10. Join the units from steps 8 and 9 to the basket unit from step 7 as shown to make a block that measures 6½" square, including seam allowances.

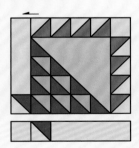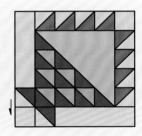

Basket of Triangles block

PRESSING MATTERS

To prevent bumpy basket seams, press the triangles and their strips in the same direction and stitch rows together so the seams meet and are not stacked on one another. Twist intersections and clip next to the seam as necessary. Finish with a good press. ◆

41 PINWHEEL STAR

by Lisa Bongean

MATERIALS

The featured block uses 2 light and 3 assorted dark prints.

A: 2 squares, 1⅞" × 1⅞", of light print #1
B: 2 squares, 1⅞" × 1⅞", of dark print #1
C: 2 squares, 2⅜" × 2⅜", of dark print #2;
    cut in half diagonally to yield 4 triangles
D: 8 squares, 2" × 2", of dark print #3
E: 4 rectangles, 2" × 3½", of light print #2
F: 4 squares, 2" × 2", of light print #2

BLOCK ASSEMBLY

Press all seam allowances in the directions indicated by the arrows.

1. Draw a diagonal line from corner to corner on the wrong side of each A square. Place a marked square right sides together with a B square. Sew ¼" from both sides of the drawn line. Cut the unit apart on the marked line to make two half-square-triangle units. Make four units that measure 1½" square, including seam allowances.

Make 4 units,
1½" × 1½".

2. Lay out the half-square-triangle units in two rows, rotating the units as shown. Sew the units together into rows. Join the rows to make a pinwheel unit that measures 2½" square, including seam allowances.

Make 1 unit,
2½" × 2½".

3. Fold the C triangles in half, and lightly crease to mark the center of the long side. Sew triangles to opposite sides of the pinwheel unit, matching the center creases to the seamline; press. Sew triangles to the remaining sides of the square to make the center unit. Square up the unit to measure 3½" square, including seam allowances.

Make 1 unit,
3½" × 3½".

4. Mark a diagonal line from corner to corner on the wrong side of the D squares. Place a marked square on one end of an E rectangle, right sides together, and stitch on the drawn line. Trim the seam allowances to ¼"; press. Place a second marked square on the opposite end of the rectangle, right sides together; stitch, trim, and press to make a flying-geese unit. Make four units that measure 2" × 3½", including seam allowances.

Make 4 units,
2" × 3½".

5. Lay out the F squares, flying-geese units, and center unit in three rows, rotating the units as shown. Sew the units and squares together into rows. Join the rows to make a block that measures 6½" square, including seam allowances.

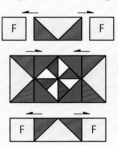 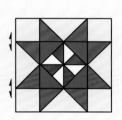

Pinwheel Star block

"

Around the Block

"Okay, I might have tweaked my block just a little bit. I used two different prints for the D triangles on the flying geese. Sometimes it's hard not to make things scrappier!"

~ CARRIE NELSON

42 SUNFLOWER

by Carrie Nelson

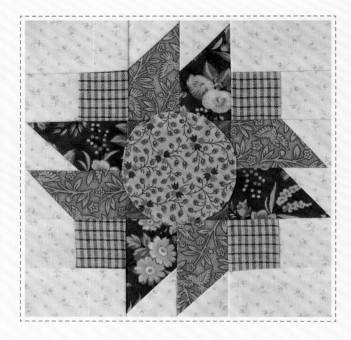

MATERIALS

The featured block uses 2 light, 1 dark, and 3 medium prints.

A: 12 squares, 1½" × 1½", of light print #1
B: 4 squares, 1½" × 1½", of medium print #1
C: 4 rectangles, 1½" × 2½", of light print #1
D: 4 rectangles, 1½" × 2½", of medium print #2
E: 4 rectangles, 1½" × 2½", of dark print
F: 1 square, 2½" × 2½", of medium print #3
G: 1 square, 2¾" × 2¾", of light print #2
Cardstock

BLOCK ASSEMBLY

Press all seam allowances in the directions indicated by the arrows.

1. Sew an A square to a B square to make a two-patch unit. Sew a C rectangle to the top of the A/B unit to make a corner unit. Make two units and two reversed units that measure 2½" square, including seam allowances.

Make 2 of each unit,
2½" × 2½".

2. Mark a diagonal line from corner to corner on the wrong side of the remaining A squares. Place a marked square on one end of a D rectangle, right sides together, making sure to orient the marked line as shown. Stitch on the drawn line. Trim the seam allowances to ¼"; press. Make four units that measure 1½" × 2½", including seam allowances.

Make 4 units,
1½" × 2½".

3. Repeat step 2 using the remaining marked A squares and the E rectangles to make four units that measure 1½" × 2½", including seam allowances.

Make 4 units,
1½" × 2½".

4. Join an A/D unit to the left side of an A/E unit to make a side unit. Make four units that measure 2½" square, including seam allowances.

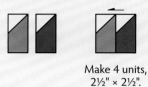

Make 4 units,
2½" × 2½".

5. Lay out the corner units, side units, and F square in three rows, rotating the units as shown. Sew the units and square together into rows. Join the rows to make a block that measures 6½" square, including seam allowances.

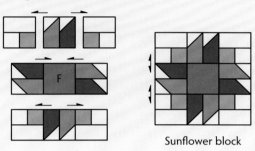

Sunflower block

6. Make a template using the circle pattern at right and cardstock. Use the template to trace the circle onto the wrong side of the G square. Cut out the circle, adding a generous ¼" seam allowance all around the perimeter.

7. Using a needle and thread, hand baste around the traced circle, sewing ⅛" from the drawn line. Place the template in the center of the fabric circle. Pull the thread to snugly gather the fabric around the template. Knot the threads. Press well. Snip the basting thread and remove the template.

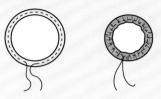

8. Center the prepared circle on the F square as shown in the photo on page 86. Stitch around the outer edge of the circle using matching thread and a straight stitch.

Pattern does not include
seam allowance.

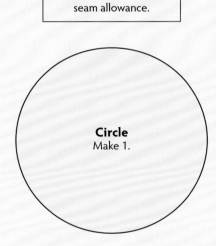

Circle
Make 1.

Quilt Blocks

43 ANY DIRECTION

by Lynne Hagmeier

MATERIALS

The featured block uses 1 light, 1 medium, and 2 dark prints.

A: 16 squares, 1½" × 1½", of light print
B: 4 rectangles, 1½" × 2½", of dark print #1
C: 4 rectangles, 1½" × 2½", of medium print
D: 8 squares, 1½" × 1½", of dark print #2
E: 5 squares, 2½" × 2½", of light print

BLOCK ASSEMBLY

Press all seam allowances in the directions indicated by the arrows.

1. Layer an A square on one end of a B rectangle, right sides together and raw edges aligned. Stitch diagonally across the A square. (You can draw a line diagonally from corner to corner or just eyeball it.) Trim the seam allowances to ¼"; press. Layer a second A square on the opposite end of the B rectangle. Sew, trim, and press as shown. Make four flying-geese units that measure 1½" × 2½", including seam allowances.

Make 4 units,
1½" × 2½".

2. Repeat step 1 using the remaining A squares and the C rectangles to make four flying-geese units that measure 1½" × 2½", including seam allowances.

Make 4 units,
1½" × 2½".

3. Sew an A/B unit to an A/C unit as shown to make a side unit. Make four units that measure 2½" square, including seam allowances.

Make 4 units,
2½" × 2½".

4. Layer a D square on one corner of an E square, right sides together and raw edges aligned. Stitch diagonally across the D square. Trim the seam allowances to ¼"; press. Repeat to sew D squares to the remaining three corners of the E square as shown to make the center unit. Make one unit that measures 2½" square, including seam allowances.

Make 1 unit,
2½" × 2½".

5. Layer a D square on one corner of an E square, right sides together and raw edges aligned. Stitch diagonally across the D square. Trim the seam allowances to ¼". Make four corner units that measure 2½" square, including seam allowances.

Make 4 units,
2½" × 2½".

6. Lay out the units from steps 3, 4, and 5 in three rows, rotating them as shown. Sew the units together into rows. Join the rows to make a block that measures 6½" square, including seam allowances.

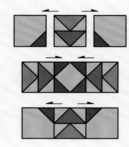 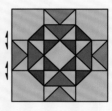

Any Direction block

44 DOUBLE DUTCH

by Jo Morton

MATERIALS

The featured block uses 2 light and 2 dark prints.

A: 16 squares, 1¼" × 1¼", of light print #1
B: 4 rectangles, 1¼" × 2", of dark print #1
C: 4 rectangles, 1¼" × 2", of dark print #2
D: 2 squares, 2⅜" × 2⅜", of light print #2
E: 2 squares, 2⅜" × 2⅜", of dark print #2
F: 8 squares, 2" × 2", of light print #2
G: 4 rectangles, 2" × 3½", of dark print #1

BLOCK ASSEMBLY

Press all seam allowances in the directions indicated by the arrows.

1. Layer an A square on one end of a B rectangle, right sides together and raw edges aligned. Stitch diagonally across the A square. (You can draw a line diagonally from corner to corner or just eyeball it.) Trim the seam allowances to ¼"; press. Place a second A square on the opposite end of the B rectangle. Sew, trim, and press as shown. Make four flying-geese units that measure 1¼" × 2", including seam allowances.

Make 4 units,
1¼" × 2".

2. Repeat step 1 using the remaining A squares and the C rectangles to make four flying-geese units that measure 1¼" × 2", including seam allowances.

Make 4 units,
1¼" × 2".

3. Join an A/B unit and an A/C unit. Make four units that measure 2" square, including seam allowances.

Make 4 units,
2" × 2".

4. Draw a diagonal line from corner to corner on the wrong side of each D square. Place a marked square right sides together with an E square. Sew ¼" from both sides of the drawn line. Cut the unit apart on the marked line to make two half-square-triangle units. Make four units that measure 2" square, including seam allowances.

Make 4 units,
2" × 2".

5. Layer an F square on one end of a G rectangle, right sides together and raw edges aligned. Stitch diagonally across the F square. Trim the seam allowances to ¼"; press. Place a second F square on the opposite end of the G rectangle. Sew, trim, and press as shown. Make four flying-geese units that measure 2" × 3½", including seam allowances.

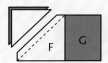 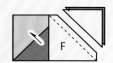

Make 4 units,
2" × 3½".

6. Lay out one unit from step 3, one half-square-triangle unit, and one F/G flying-geese unit as shown. Join the units to make a quarter-block unit. Make four units that measure 3½" square, including seam allowances.

Make 4 units,
3½" × 3½".

7. Lay out the quarter-block units in two rows, rotating them as shown. Sew the units together into rows. Join the rows to make a block that measures 6½" square, including seam allowances.

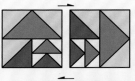 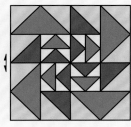

Double Dutch block

Quilt Blocks

45 CARDINAL

by Jan Patek

MATERIALS

The featured block uses 1 light, 1 dark, and 4 medium prints.

1 rectangle, 2¼" × 5½", of medium print #1 for branch

1 square, 1¾" × 1¾", of medium print #2 for berry

2 rectangles, 1¼" × 2¼", of medium print #3 for leaves

1 rectangle, 2¾" × 4¼", of medium print #2 for bird

1 rectangle, 1½" × 2¼", of medium print #4 for bird's wing

1 rectangle, 2½" × 3", of light print for star

1 square, 7" × 7", of dark print for background

Embroidery floss

Freezer paper

Appliqué glue (optional)

BLOCK ASSEMBLY

The instructions are written for needle-turn appliqué, which Jan used, but use your favorite method if you prefer. All the appliqué patterns are on page 93. Reverse the patterns for fusible appliqué.

1. Trace the branch, berry, leaves, bird, bird's wing, and star onto the dull side of the freezer paper. Cut out the templates directly on the line.

2. Place each freezer-paper template on the right side of the appropriate fabric, shiny side down. Press in place.

3. Trace around the templates. Cut out the fabric shapes, adding ¼" seam allowance all around. Remove the freezer-paper template.

4. Pin, baste, or glue the pieces to the background, starting with the branch. Appliqué in place. Add the berry, leaves, bird, and then the bird's wing. Appliqué the star in place.

Appliqué placement diagram

5. Embroider the bird's eye using two strands of embroidery floss and a stem stitch (see page 20).

6. Press the block on the wrong side and trim it to 6½" square, keeping the design centered.

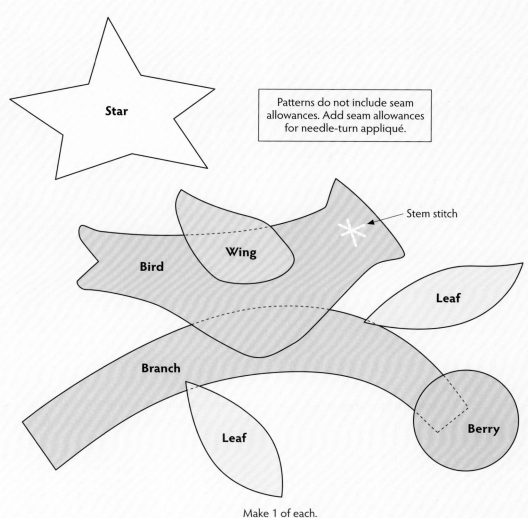

Star

Patterns do not include seam allowances. Add seam allowances for needle-turn appliqué.

Stem stitch

Wing

Bird

Leaf

Branch

Leaf

Berry

Make 1 of each.

Around the Block

"There's no wrong way to appliqué. While Jan does turned-edge appliqué, you could also try fusible appliqué. Or imagine wool appliqués stitched to a cotton background using a blanket stitch. A good reminder to make your block your own."
~ Lynne Hagmeier

46 STARRY NINE PATCH

by Lisa Bongean

MATERIALS

The featured block uses 1 light, 1 medium, and 1 dark print.

A: 4 squares, 1½" × 1½", of dark print

B: 4 squares, 1½" × 1½", of light print

C: 1 square, 1½" × 1½", of medium print

D: 2 squares, 2¾" × 2¾", of dark print; cut into quarters diagonally to yield 8 triangles

E: 2 squares, 2¾" × 2¾", of medium print; cut into quarters diagonally to yield 8 triangles

F: 1 square, 4¼" × 4¼", of light print; cut into quarters diagonally to yield 4 triangles

G: 4 squares, 2" × 2", of light print

BLOCK ASSEMBLY

Press all seam allowances in the directions indicated by the arrows.

1. Sew together two A squares and one B square. Make two units that measure 1½" × 3½", including seam allowances.

Make 2 units,
1½" × 3½".

2. Sew together two B squares and one C square. Make one unit that measures 1½" × 3½", including seam allowances.

Make 1 unit,
1½" × 3½".

3. Lay out the units from steps 1 and 2 as shown. Join the units to make a nine-patch unit that measures 3½" square, including seam allowances.

Make 1 unit,
3½" × 3½".

4. Sew a D triangle to an E triangle to make a pieced triangle unit. Make four units and four reversed units.

Make 4 of each unit.

5. Sew a triangle unit and a reversed triangle unit from step 4 to the short sides of an F triangle to make a side unit. Make four units that measure 2" × 3½", including seam allowances.

Make 4 units,
2" × 3½".

6. Lay out the G squares, side units, and nine-patch unit in three rows, rotating the side units as shown. Sew the units and squares together into rows. Join the rows to make a block that measures 6½" square, including seam allowances.

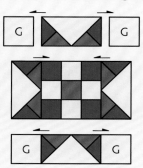 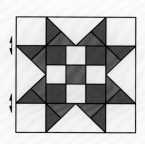

Starry Nine Patch block

Quilt Blocks

47 HONEYMOON

by Carrie Nelson

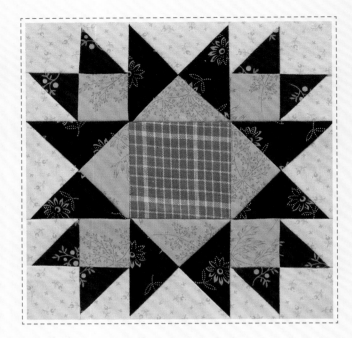

MATERIALS

The featured block uses 1 light, 2 medium, and 2 dark prints.

A: 4 squares, 1⅞" × 1⅞", of light print

B: 4 squares, 1⅞" × 1⅞", of dark print #1

C: 4 squares, 1½" × 1½", of light print

D: 4 squares, 1½" × 1½", of medium print #1

E: 2 squares, 3¼" × 3¼", of dark print #2; cut into quarters diagonally to yield 8 triangles

F: 1 square, 3¼" × 3¼", of light print; cut into quarters diagonally to yield 4 triangles

G: 1 square, 3¼" × 3¼", of medium print #1; cut into quarters diagonally to yield 4 triangles

H: 1 square, 2½" × 2½", of medium print #2

BLOCK ASSEMBLY

Press all seam allowances in the directions indicated by the arrows.

1. Draw a line from corner to corner on the wrong side of each A square. Place a marked square right sides together with a B square. Sew ¼" from both sides of the drawn line. Cut on the line to make two half-square-triangle units. Make eight units measuring 1½" square, including seam allowances.

Make 8 units, 1½" × 1½".

2. Join one C square, two half-square-triangle units, and one D square as shown above right to make a corner unit. Make four units that measure 2½" square, including seam allowances.

Make 4 units, 2½" × 2½".

3. Join two E, one F, and one G triangle as shown to make an hourglass unit. Make four units that measure 2½" square, including seam allowances.

Make 4 units, 2½" × 2½".

4. Sew the units and H square together into rows. Join the rows to make a block that measures 6½" square, including seam allowances.

Honeymoon block

Moda Blockheads

48 PEACE AND PLENTY

by Betsy Chutchian

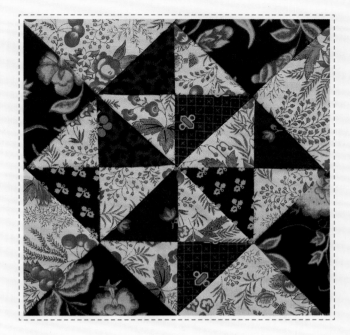

MATERIALS

The featured block uses 1 light and 5 assorted dark prints (4 dark prints are collectively referred to as dark print #1; the other is dark print #2).

A: 2 squares, 3⅜" × 3⅜", of light print; cut into quarters diagonally to yield 8 triangles

B: 4 squares, 3⅜" × 3⅜", of dark print #1; cut into quarters diagonally to yield 16 triangles (2 triangles from each print will be extra)

C: 1 square, 4¼" × 4¼", of dark print #2; cut into quarters diagonally to yield 4 triangles

D: 1 square, 4¼" × 4¼", of light print; cut into quarters diagonally to yield 4 triangles

BLOCK ASSEMBLY

Press all seam allowances in the directions indicated by the arrows.

1. Join two A and two B triangles as shown to make an hourglass unit. Make four units that measure 2⅝" square, including seam allowances.

Make 4 units,
2⅝" × 2⅝".

2. Sew the hourglass units together as shown to make a center unit that measures 4¾" square, including seam allowances.

Make 1 unit,
4¾" × 4¾".

3. Join C and D triangles along one short side to make a pieced triangle unit. Make four units.

Make 4 units.

4. Sew triangle units to opposite sides of the center unit; press. Sew triangle units to the remaining two sides to make a block that measures 6½" square, including seam allowances.

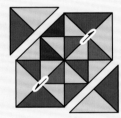 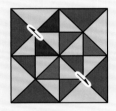

Peace and Plenty block

Quilt Plans

BETSY'S
BLOCKHEAD QUILT

Pieced by Betsy Chutchian; machine quilted by Maggi Honeyman

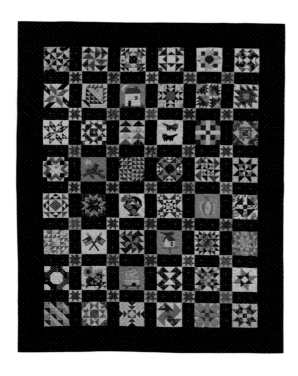

FINISHED BLOCKS: 6" × 6"

FINISHED QUILT: 64" × 82"

MATERIALS

You'll need 48 blocks, 6" square. All other materials are based on 42"-wide fabric, unless otherwise noted.

35 scraps, 3" × 13", of assorted red prints for sashing stars

35 scraps, 3" × 6", of assorted yellow prints for sashing stars

3¾ yards of navy print for sashing, borders, and binding

5 yards of backing fabric

72" × 90" piece of batting

CUTTING

From *each* red scrap, cut:

1 square, 2" × 2" (35 total)

4 squares, 1¾" × 1¾" (140 total)

From *each* yellow scrap, cut:

1 square, 2⅞" × 2⅞" (35 total)

4 squares, 1¼" × 1¼" (140 total)

From the navy print, cut:

7 strips, 6¾" × 42"

8 strips, 6½" × 42"; crosscut into 82 rectangles, 3½" × 6½"

8 strips, 2½" × 42"

MAKING THE SASHING STARS

Pair the pieces from one red print and one yellow print for each star. Note that cutting is slightly oversized to allow for trimming down. Instructions are for making one star; repeat to make 35 stars. Press all seam allowances in the direction of the arrows.

1. To make the star points, mark a diagonal line from corner to corner on the wrong side of the red 1¾" squares. Place a square on one corner of a yellow 2⅞" square. Place another red square on the diagonally opposite corner. Sew a scant ¼" from each side of the marked lines, cut apart on the marked lines, and press.

2. Place a marked red square on the remaining square corner of each unit from step 1. Stitch a scant ¼" from each side of the line, cut apart, and press open. You'll have a total of four matching flying-geese units. Trim each to 1¼" × 2", including seam allowances.

Make 140 units.

3. Lay out four star-point units, a red 2" square, and four yellow 1¼" squares as shown. Sew the pieces together in rows and then join the rows. Press. The completed star should be 3½" square, including seam allowances. Repeat steps 1–3 to make a total of 35 sashing stars.

Make 35 sashing stars,
3½" × 3½".

QUILT ASSEMBLY

1. Lay out the blocks in eight rows of six blocks each. Place the navy sashing rectangles between the blocks, both horizontally and vertically. Place a sashing star at the intersection of each sashing row.

2. Sew the blocks and sashing pieces together in rows. Press. Sew the sashing stars and rectangles together in rows. Press. Each row should be 51½" long.

3. Join the rows to complete the quilt top center, which should be 51½" × 69½".

4. Sew the navy 6¾"-wide strips together end to end. Press and then from this long strip, cut two border strips, 69½" long, and two strips, 64" long.

5. Sew the long strips to the sides of the quilt top; press. Sew the shorter strips to the top and bottom of the quilt top; press.

6. Layer, baste, and quilt. Betsy's quilt is machine quilted with a pumpkin seed design in the sashing and outline quilting around the pieces in the blocks.

7. Use the navy 2½" strips to make double-fold binding. Attach the binding to the quilt.

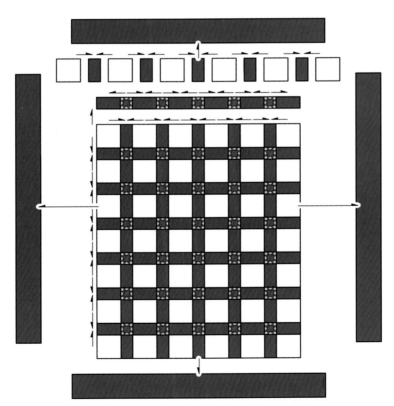

Quilt assembly

JO'S BLOCKHEAD QUILT

Pieced by Jo Morton; machine quilted by Maggi Honeyman

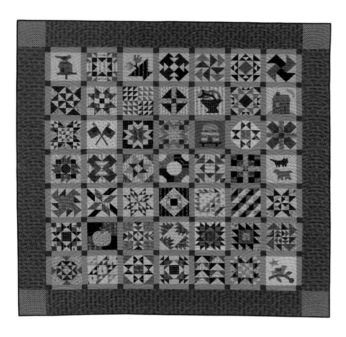

FINISHED BLOCKS: 6" × 6"
FINISHED QUILT: 62½" × 62½"

MATERIALS

You'll need 49 blocks, 6" square. (Jo made two of block 12 on page 36.) Yardage is based on 42"-wide fabric; fat quarters are 18" × 21".

1 yard of tan print A for sashing strips
1 fat quarter of red print for sashing cornerstones
1⅛ yards of blue stripe for border
1 fat quarter of tan print B for border corners
¼ yard of navy print for single-fold binding
3⅞ yards of backing fabric
69" × 69" piece of batting

CUTTING

From tan print A, cut:
5 strips, 6½" × 42"; crosscut into 112 strips, 1⅝" × 6½"

From the red print, cut:
6 strips, 1⅝" × 21"; crosscut into 64 squares, 1⅝" × 1⅝"

From the blue stripe, cut:
6 strips, 6" × 42"; cut *2 of the strips* in half to yield 4 strips, 6" × 21"

From tan print B, cut:
1 strip, 6" × 21"; crosscut into 4 squares, 6" × 6"

From the navy print, cut:
7 strips, 1⅛" × 42", for single-fold binding

QUILT ASSEMBLY

Press all seam allowances in the direction of the arrows.

1. Lay out the blocks in seven rows of seven blocks each. Place a tan A sashing strip between the blocks as well as on both ends of each row. Between block rows, lay out the remaining sashing strips and the red sashing squares.

2. Join the pieces in each row and press. Then join the rows. Press.

ASSEMBLE IN QUADRANTS

Rather than sewing so many long rows, I prefer to assemble my quilt tops in smaller chunks. You can divide the quilt top (roughly) into quarters, assemble each quadrant, and then join the quadrants. The only long seam will be the last one. ◆

3. Sew each of the blue half-border strips to one of the full-length border strips to make four borders that are each 51½" long. Pin a border strip to one side of the quilt, pinning at the ends and the midpoint, easing in any discrepancy. Sew the border to the quilt and then repeat on the opposite side.

4. Sew tan print B squares to both ends of the two remaining border strips. Pin and then sew these to the top and bottom of the quilt top. Press. The quilt top should measure 62½" square.

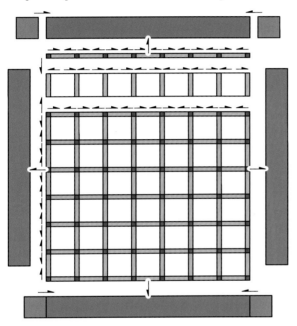

Quilt assembly

5. Layer, baste, and quilt. Jo's quilt is machine quilted with a Baptist fan pattern that runs vertically from edge to edge, rather than the more common diagonal version.

6. Join the navy binding strips end to end with a diagonal seam. Press the seam allowances open. Sew the binding to the quilt, mitering the corners as you go. For more information on single-fold binding, go to ShopMartingale.com/HowtoQuilt; the binding section has free illustrated details.

CARRIE'S
BLOCKHEAD QUILT

**Pieced by Carrie Nelson; machine quilted by
Carrie Straka of Red Velvet Quilts**

FINISHED BLOCKS: 6" × 6"

FINISHED QUILT: 78½" × 78½"

MATERIALS

You'll need 64 blocks, 6" square. Yardage is based on 42"-wide fabric; fat quarters are 18" × 21".

2¼ yards *total* of assorted prints for flying-geese sashing (options include 28 Layer Cake squares, 20 fat eighths, or 10 fat quarters in lieu of scraps)

5 yards of light print for background

¾ yard of blue print for binding (or 2½"-wide strips of assorted blues and reds)

7⅛ yards of backing fabric

85" × 85" piece of batting

CUTTING

From the assorted prints, cut:

113 squares, 4½" × 4½"

From the light print, cut:

33 strips, 2¾" × 42"; crosscut into 452 squares, 2¾" × 2¾", for flying-geese units

35 strips, 1½" × 42"; crosscut as follows:
  From 3 strips, cut 16 rectangles, 1½" × 6½"
  From 16 strips, cut 48 rectangles, 1½" × 13½"
  From *each* of the remaining 16 strips, cut
    2 rectangles, 1½" × 15½", and 1 rectangle, 1½" × 6½"

1 strip, 15½" × 42"; crosscut into 16 rectangles, 2" × 15½". From the remainder of the strip, cut:
  4 rectangles, 2" × 15½"; crosscut into 16 rectangles, 2" × 3½"

1 strip, 2" × 42"; crosscut into 3 rectangles, 2" × 3½", and 4 squares, 2" × 2"

From the blue print, cut:

9 strips, 2½" × 42"

QUILT ASSEMBLY

Press all seam allowances in the direction of the arrows.

1. The blocks are joined in groups of four, separated by 1½"-wide sashing. Lay out four blocks, two 1½" × 6½" sashing strips, three 1½" × 13½" sashing strips, and two 1½" × 15½" sashing strips as shown. Join the blocks and sashing into rows; join the rows. The completed

block group should measure 15½" square. Make 16 of these block groups.

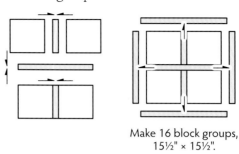

Make 16 block groups,
15½" × 15½".

2. To make the sashing, mark a diagonal line from corner to corner on the wrong side of the light 2¾" squares. Place a square on one corner of a print 4½" square. Place another light square on the diagonally opposite corner. Sew a scant ¼" from each side of the marked lines, cut apart on the marked lines, and press.

3. Place a marked light square on the remaining square corner of each unit from step 2. Stitch a scant ¼" from each side of the line, cut apart, and press open. You'll have a total of four matching flying-geese units. Trim each to 2" × 3½", including seam allowances. Repeat steps 2 and 3 to make a total of 452 flying-geese units. (You'll have one extra unit.)

Make 452 units.

4. Join two flying-geese units as shown to make a corner unit that measures 3½" square. Make 25.

Make 25 units,
3½" × 3½".

5. To make the sashing units, lay out 10 assorted flying-geese units in a row, with five pointing to the left and five pointing to the right as shown. Press. Make 21 units that measure 3½" × 15½".

Make 21 units, 3½" × 15½".

6. Join nine flying-geese units and one light 2" × 3½" rectangle as shown. Make 19 units that measure 3½" × 15½".

Make 17 units, 3½" × 15½".

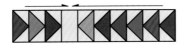

Make 2 units, 3½" × 15½".

7. Referring to the quilt assembly diagram below, lay out the block groups in four rows of four. Place a flying-geese sashing strip between the blocks both horizontally and vertically. Place the corner units at the flying-geese intersections. Sew the pieces together in rows, and then join the rows.

8. To complete the design, join five flying-geese units and four 2" × 15½" sashing strips. Make four of these border strips measuring 2" × 75½". Sew one to opposite sides of the quilt. Press. Add a light 2" square to each end of the remaining border strips and join these to the top and bottom of the quilt. The completed quilt should measure 78½" square.

9. Layer, baste, and quilt. Carrie's quilt is machine quilted with an allover swirl design.

10. Join the blue strips end to end with a diagonal seam to make double-fold binding. Attach the binding to your quilt.

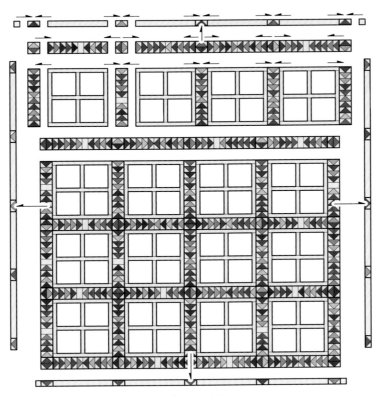

Quilt assembly

JAN'S BLOCKHEAD QUILT

Pieced and appliquéd by Jan Patek; machine quilted by Lori Kukuk

FINISHED BLOCKS: 6" × 6"

CENTER APPLIQUÉ BLOCK: 18" × 18"

FINISHED QUILT: 54½" × 60½"

MATERIALS

You'll need 48 blocks, 6" square. Yardage is based on 42"-wide fabric; fat quarters are 18" × 21".

20" × 20" piece of cream print for center appliqué block background

6" × 20" piece of green plaid for center appliqué block background

Scraps of assorted prints and plaids for house, trees, bird, stars, and moon for center appliqué block

1⅝ yards of dark red print for borders

¼ yard of cream print for strip of appliquéd stars

8" × 8" square *each* of 2 tan prints for cornerstones

8" × 8" square *each* of blue and red prints for appliquéd stars

½ yard of navy print for binding

3½" yards of fabric for backing

61" × 67" piece of batting

CUTTING

From the cream print for strip of stars, cut:

1 strip, 6½" × 24½"

From *each* of the tan 8" squares, cut:

4 squares, 3½" × 3½" (8 total)

From the dark red print, cut on the *lengthwise* grain:

2 strips, 3½" × 54½"

2 strips, 3½" × 48½"

4 strips, 3½" × 30½"

From the navy print, cut:

6 strips, 2½" × 42"

QUILT ASSEMBLY

The center of this quilt features an 18" square appliquéd block. The patterns for this block and for the small and large appliquéd stars are online at ShopMartingale.com/ModaBlockheads. Press all seam allowances in the direction of the arrows.

1. Appliqué the center block design or one of your own choosing onto the 20" cream square, then trim to 18½" square. Or, substitute with nine 6" blocks.

2. Appliqué eight cornerstone blocks with small stars (four red and four blue) using the online pattern and the 3½" tan squares. Also appliqué the cream 6½" × 24½" strip with four large stars using the online pattern and assorted print scraps.

3. Referring to the quilt assembly diagram on page 107, lay out the 6" quilt blocks, red border strips, and appliquéd star strip and squares around the center appliqué block. (Note that Jan placed her 6" appliqué blocks in the corners of each round of quilt blocks.) Join the three blocks above the center appliqué block and sew the row to the top of the block. Repeat for the three blocks below the center appliqué block.

4. Join the five blocks on each side of the center appliqué block into vertical strips and sew them to the sides of the quilt center.

5. Sew red 3½" × 30½" strips to the sides of the quilt center; press. Join a blue Star block to each end of the remaining red 3½" × 30½" strips and sew them to the top and bottom of the quilt center. Press.

6. Join the six blocks above the red border and sew them to the top of the quilt. Repeat for the six blocks below the bottom red border. Sew a 6" block

to each end of the 6½" × 24½" star strip and sew it to the top of the quilt center. Press. Join the nine blocks on each side of the quilt center into vertical strips and sew them to the sides of the quilt center. Press.

7. Sew the red 3½" × 54½" strips to the sides of the quilt; press. Sew a red Star block to each end of the red 3½" × 48½" strips and sew these to the top and bottom of the quilt center. Press.

8. Layer, baste, and quilt. Jan's quilt is machine quilted with meandering in the center appliqué block, diagonal crosshatching in the borders, and custom quilting in the individual 6" blocks.

9. Join the navy strips end to end with a diagonal seam to make double-fold binding. Attach the binding to your quilt.

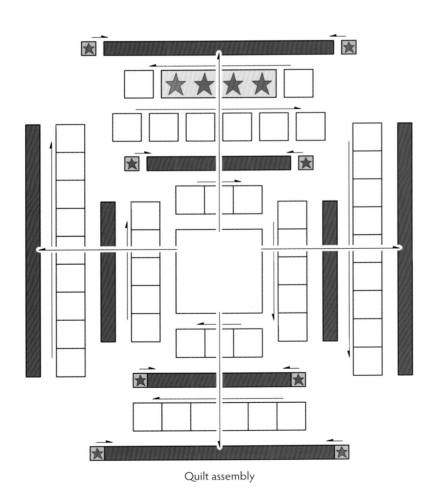

Quilt assembly

LISA'S
BLOCKHEAD QUILT

Pieced by Lisa Bongean; machine quilted by Linda Hrcka

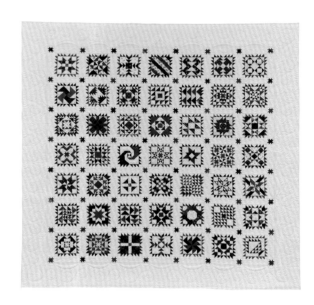

FINISHED BLOCKS: 6" × 6"
FINISHED QUILT: 88½" × 88½"

MATERIALS

You'll need 49 blocks, 6" square. (Lisa substituted the 8 appliqué blocks in this book with patchwork blocks.) Yardage is based on 42"-wide fabric; fat eighths are 9" × 21".

8⅝ yards of cream solid for block frames, sashing, sashing stars, border, and binding

13 fat eighths of assorted red prints for block frames and sashing stars

12 fat eighths of assorted navy prints for block frames and sashing squares

8 yards of fabric for backing

97" × 97" piece of batting

2 packages of Primitive Gatherings 1" Finished Triangle Paper for piecing the block frames

Fabric starch (optional)

CUTTING

Lisa recommends starch to tame small pieces. Let the starch dry and then press before cutting so that it doesn't distort the fabric after it's cut.

From the cream solid, cut:

13 strips, 6" × 42"; cut in 49 rectangles, 6" × 9"

17 strips, 1" × 42"; cut into:
    256 rectangles, 1" × 1½"
    256 squares, 1" × 1"

8 strips, 1½" × 42"; cut into 196 squares, 1½" × 1½"

7 strips, 8½" × 42"; cut into 112 sashing strips, 2½" × 8½"

10 strips, 2½" × 42", for binding

From the remaining cream solid, cut on the *lengthwise* grain:

2 strips, 8½" × 72½"

2 strips, 8½" × 88½"

From the assorted red prints, cut:

25 rectangles, 6" × 9"

32 matching sets of: 1 square, 1½" × 1½", and 8 squares, 1" × 1"

From the assorted navy prints, cut:

24 rectangles, 6" × 9"

32 matching sets of: 1 square, 1½" × 1½", and 8 squares, 1" × 1"

FRAMING THE BLOCKS

1. Layer a red and a cream 6" × 9" rectangle right sides together. Place a 1" finished triangle paper on top of the cream fabric and pin in place. Following the instructions on the package, sew on the marked lines and then cut apart on the lines indicated. Repeat, pairing each red and navy rectangle with a cream one, to make a total of 24 half-square-triangle units per block (600 red total; 576 navy total). Press the resulting units open and remove the paper.

Make 600 red units, 1½" × 1½".

Make 576 navy units, 1½" × 1½".

2. Lay out 24 matching half-square-triangle units around a patchwork block, placing a cream 1½" square at each corner. Sew the units together in rows. Sew one row to the top of the block and one row to the bottom. Add the cream squares to the ends of the remaining two rows and sew these to the sides of the block. Press. The framed block should measure 8½" square, including the seam allowances.

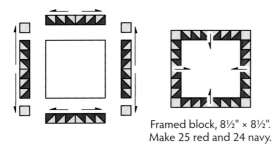

Framed block, 8½" × 8½".
Make 25 red and 24 navy.

3. Repeat steps 1 and 2, making 25 blocks with red frames and 24 blocks with navy frames.

MAKING THE SASHING STARS

For each star, gather one set of matching red or navy pieces (one 1½" square and eight 1" squares) plus four cream rectangles, 1" × 1½", and four cream 1" squares.

1. Mark a diagonal line from corner to corner on the wrong side of the red 1" squares; however, they're so small that you can eyeball the diagonal if you prefer. Place a red square on one end of a cream rectangle and sew exactly on the drawn line. Trim away the excess corner fabric, leaving a ¼" seam allowance. Repeat on the opposite end to make a flying-geese unit. Press. Repeat to make four matching units.

Make 4 matching units,
1" × 1½".

2. Lay out the four flying-geese units, the matching red 1½" square, and four cream

1" squares in three rows. Join the pieces in each row, then join the rows. Press. The completed sashing star should measure 2½" square, including seam allowances. Repeat to make a total of 32 red stars and 32 navy stars.

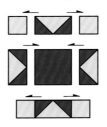

Make 32 red and
32 navy stars, 2½" × 2½".

ASSEMBLING THE QUILT TOP

1. Lay out the pieced blocks in seven rows of seven blocks each, starting with a red framed block in the corners and alternating between red and blue frames.

2. Place the cream sashing strips and sashing stars in between the block rows. Join the pieces in each row; press. Join the rows; press. The quilt top should measure 72½" square, including seam allowances.

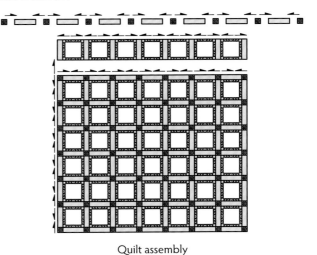

Quilt assembly

3. Join the cream 72½" strips to the sides of the quilt top; press. Sew the cream 88½" strips to the top and bottom of the quilt top; press.

LYNNE'S
BLOCKHEAD QUILT

Pieced by Lynne Hagmeier; machine quilted by Joy Johnson of Joyful Quilting.

FINISHED BLOCKS: 6" × 6"
FINISHED QUILT: 102½" × 108½"

MATERIALS

You'll need 50 blocks, 6" square, plus 4 of the Dutchman's Puzzle block (page 67). Yardage is based on 42"-wide fabric.

¼ yard *each* of 6 assorted prints in *each* of the following colors: navy, olive, gold, plum, blue, and dark red OR 1 Layer Cake (40 squares, 10" × 10") of dark prints for setting squares and pieced border

2⅔ yards of dark red print for borders #1 and #5

1⅝ yards of gold print for border #2

2⅓ yards of tan print for borders #3 and #4

4 yards of navy print for border #6 and binding

10 yards of fabric for backing

120" × 120" piece of batting

CUTTING

From *each* of the assorted blue, olive, plum, gold, and navy prints, cut:
1 square, 6½" × 6½" (30 total)

From the assorted dark red prints, cut a total of:
6 squares, 9¾" × 9¾"; cut the squares diagonally into quarters to yield 24 triangles (2 will be extra)
2 squares, 5¼" × 5¼"; cut the squares in half diagonally to yield 4 triangles

From the remainder of the assorted blue, plum, olive, gold, navy, and red prints, cut a total of:
52 squares, 3½" × 3½"; cut squares in half diagonally to yield 104 triangles for layered patchwork border

From the dark red yardage, cut on the *lengthwise* grain:
2 strips, 2½" × 60"
2 strips, 2" × 55½"
2 strips, 2½" × 82½"
2 strips, 2½" × 84½"

From the gold yardage, cut on the *lengthwise* grain:
2 strips, 6½" × 43½"
2 strips, 6½" × 51½"

From the tan yardage, cut on the *lengthwise* grain:
2 strips, 3" × 75"
2 strips, 2¼" × 72½"
6 strips, 3½" × length of fabric; crosscut into:
    48 rectangles, 3½" × 6½"
    8 squares, 3½" × 3½"

From the navy print, cut:
11 strips, 2¼" × 42", for binding

From the remaining navy print, cut on the *lengthwise* grain:
2 strips, 10" × 88½"
2 strips, 10" × 102½"

ASSEMBLING THE QUILT

Refer to the quilt assembly diagram as needed. Press the seam allowances in the direction of the arrows.

1. Choose 42 of the 6" blocks for the quilt center and lay them out on point in six columns of seven blocks each. Place the 6½" print squares between the blocks so they form columns of individual colors: blue, plum, gold, olive, and navy.

2. Place the large red triangles around the perimeter of the blocks and the small red triangles in the corners. Join the blocks and triangles in diagonal rows. Join the rows. The quilt center should measure 51½" × 60".

3. Join the dark red 2½" × 60" strips to the sides of the quilt top. Sew the 2" × 55½" dark red strips to the top and bottom.

4. Sew one of the appliqué blocks to the each end of each of the 6½" wide gold border strips. (Pay attention to the direction of the appliqué blocks so they all appear upright in the finished quilt.) Sew the longer borders to the sides of the quilt. Sew a Dutchman's Puzzle block to each end of the shorter gold borders and sew them to the top and bottom of the quilt top. **Note:** For the Dutchman Puzzle blocks, Lynne used red and blue flying geese, with the red always on top and the blue always on the bottom, positioning the units with the blue goose always at the outside edge of the block for an interesting twist on this block.

5. Join the 3"-wide tan borders to the sides of the quilt and the 2¼"-wide tan strips to the top and bottom. The quilt top should now measure 72½" × 78½", which is important so that the pieced border will fit accurately.

6. For the pieced border, layer a blue, olive, gold, plum, navy, or red triangle on each end of a tan 3½" × 6½" rectangle as shown. (A dab of glue stitck will hold them in place.) Stitch close to the diagonal edges as shown. Leave the remaining edges unsewn; they will be sew into the seam allowances when the units are joined. Make 24 A units and 24 B units. In the same manner, layer the remaining colored triangles onto tan 3½" squares and sew along the diagonal. Make eight units.

Unit A. Make 24.   Unit B. Make 24.   Layered square. Make 8.

7. Join six A and six B units to make a top border with the diagonal slant of the units changing direction at the center. (See the quilt assembly diagram.) Make two. The borders should measure 72½" long; sew them to the quilt top and bottom.

8. For the side borders, join six A and six B units, with two layered-square units in the center and one square unit on each end, paying attention to the slant of the diagonals. Make two side borders, each 3½" × 84½", and sew them to the quilt.

9. To complete the quilt top, sew the dark red 84½"-long strips to the sides of the quilt and the 82½"-long strips to the top and bottom. Sew the navy 10"-wide strips to the quilt in the same manner. The completed quilt top should measure 102½" × 108½".

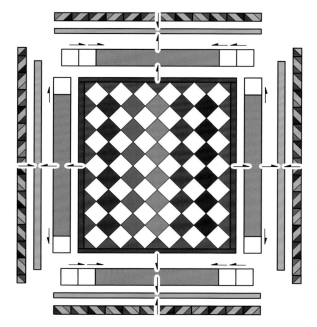

Quilt assembly

Meet the Contributors

LISA BONGEAN

A designer for Moda Fabrics, Lisa loves quilting, gardening, reading, and hunting for antiques. She and her husband, Nick, own Primitive Gatherings Quilt Shop and travel to quilting shows where Lisa teaches and shares her designs. You can find her at LisaBongean.com.

BETSY CHUTCHIAN

Betsy is an author, a designer for Moda Fabrics, and the cofounder of the 19th-Century Patchwork Divas, a block-exchange group. She developed a passionate interest in fabric, quilts, sewing, and history as a child. She enjoys sharing her love for reproducing 19th-century quilts. Visit BetsysBestQuiltsandMore.blogspot.com.

LYNNE HAGMEIER

A passion for vintage quilts inspired Lynne to take her first quilting class in 1987. Working in a quilt shop and stitching small quilts to sell led to selling patterns for the quilts she designed. Lynne has been designing popular fabric lines for Moda Fabrics since 2000. Visit her at KTQuilts.com.

JO MORTON

Jo is a celebrated author, Moda fabric designer, and teacher who is known for making present-day quilts look like quilts from the past. Well known for her "Jo's Little Women Club" patterns, she is the author of *Jo's Little Favorites* (Martingale, 2016). Visit her at JoMortonQuilts.com.

CARRIE NELSON

Carrie's fans know her by her pattern-designer name, Miss Rosie. At Moda, Carrie is the guru of social media (perhaps not her official title, but that's what she's all about), but she still slips into her Miss Rosie mode from time to time. No matter what you call her, you'll call her patchwork patterns brilliant!

JAN PATEK

Jan is a designer for Moda Fabrics who has been creating primitive folk-art quilts for more than 20 years. To meet the demand for her quilt and fabric designs, she began turning them into kits. Jan is motivated by a desire to inspire others to have a creative outlet. Find her at JanPatekQuilts.com and visit her blog at JanPatek.blogspot.com.